THINGS
WE
ADORE

How to Recognize and Get Free of Idolatry

THINGS
WE
ADORE

How to Recognize and Get Free of Idolatry

by
Judson Cornwall, Th.D.

Destiny Image Publishers
P.O. Box 310
Shippensburg, PA 17257

"Speaking to the Purposes of God for this Generation"

Library of Congress Catalog Card Number: 91-074143
ISBN 1-56043-048-6

For Worldwide Distribution
Printed in the U.S.A.

First Printing: 1991
Second Printing: 1995

Destiny Image books are available through these fine distributors outside the United States:

Christian Growth, Inc.
Jalan Kilang-Timor, Singapore 0315

Successful Christian Living
Capetown, Rep. of South Africa

Lifestream
Nottingham, England

Vision Resources
Ponsonby, Auckland, New Zealand

Rhema Ministries Trading
Randburg, South Africa

WA Buchanan Company
Geebung, Queensland, Australia

Salvation Book Centre
Petaling, Jaya, Malaysia

Word Alive
Niverville, Manitoba, Canada

Inside the U.S., call toll free to order:
1-800-722-6774

Dedication

To Harry and Michael Jackson,
my son and daughter in the Lord.

Acknowledgments

Without the gentle prodding of my secretary, Terri Gargis, this book might never have been written. Her long hours transcribing the tapes made in conferences where this truth was preached convinced her it should be made available to the broader public.

Table of Contents

Altars are tools of expression — Altars are places of revelation — Altars often give a visual representation of the deity — God's altar pictures His provision, not His person — Altars reveal the concept of the worshiper — Altars are consistent with Scripture — God's monopoly was exchanged for multiplicity of altars

Idolatry originated in Eden — Abraham was God's third attempt to establish pure worship — Close association with idolaters breeds idolatry — The commerce of Egypt introduced idolatry — The culture of Canaan inspired idolatry — Education indoctrinated the Hebrews in idolatry — Training instilled a disposition to idolatry

Response to mystery — Request for provision — Reaching for guidance — Relationship with a higher being —

Reaction to convenience — Reverting to carnality — Religious sinning

Chapter 4
The Potency of the Things We Adore
Worship is inherent to people — Conforming to Christ is God's goal for worshipers — All worshipers conform to the object they worship — Worship conformity is demonstrated in idolatry — The Bible clearly supports this principle

Chapter 5
Israel's Pattern for Idolatry
Israel's progression into idolatry — A learned experience — Walking in heathen statutes — Secret sinning — Misplaced worship — Serving idols — Refusing to listen to God

Chapter 6
The Progression of Israel at Altars for Sinning
Israel replaced God's covenants — Israel replaced the worship of God — Israel replaced God

Chapter 7
The Perversity of Israel
Israel worshiped creation instead of the Creator — Israel traded love for lust — Israel violated the sanctity of life — Israel replaced worship with witchcraft — Israel exchanged righteousness for evil

Chapter 8
The Penalty Israel Paid for Worshiping Idols
Israel disappeared from God's sight — Israel experienced permanent rejection — Israel's enemies ravished the nation mercilessly

Chapter 9
The Pattern of Judah's Idol Worship
Judah's relationship to Israel — Judah embraces Israel's law — Judah flirts with Israel's lusts — Judah follows Israel's idolatry — Judah experienced Israel's punishment

Preface

Because travel is so much more widely available in our generation, many of us Christians are able to visit the Orient. As we stand before the great pagodas containing the golden images of Buddha, we cry, "Idolatry." While photographing the ornate cathedrals in Europe with their statues and icons, we whisper, "Idolatry." Even when we stay home and watch television, we see people celebrating religious holidays by parading with images of their gods on their shoulders. Almost involuntarily we say, "Idolatry."

Somehow we have little difficulty defining idolatry in other cultures, but we remain blind to the idolatry that is so rampant in our culture. Idolatry is polluting the worship of our modern churches throughout the western world. Whether those congregations meet in traditional style buildings with stained glass windows and pipe organs or in simpler settings with no windows and where the guitar has replaced the organ, it is unlikely they have escaped the inroads of idolatry.

The idolatry of our modern churches is devilishly dangerous, for it is neither open nor complete. Instead, it conceals itself by blending in with true worship. We have so Christianized doctrines of demons that preachers now teach them as new revelations from God. Popular leaders in religious circles receive the adulation that belongs to God. Sensuality and immorality are more than tolerated, they wear religious cloaks. How could the modern Church, especially the arm of the Church that so recently enjoyed a vital visitation of God's presence, so quickly embrace idolatry? It cannot be because of disappointment with God. I find it hard to believe that carnal and sensual desires are so strong that people would willingly exchange a relationship with God for the fulfillment of their lower nature. No, there must be something stronger than this behind the change.

Paul, in reviewing some of Israel's failures, wrote: "Now all these things happened to them as examples, and they were written for our admonition, on whom the ends of the ages have come" (1 Corinthians 10:11). Israel benefited from God's provisions as much or more than any of us, and yet that nation turned from God to idols. Later, Judah, in spite of seeing what happened to Israel, also turned to idolatry.

During a series of conferences in England, I reread the Old Testament. I began to see the pattern of Israel's departure into idolatry and the contrast of Judah's walk into idolatry. Upon my return to America, I taught what I had seen with positive response. During the following two years, I received more requests to have that series put into book form than any other series of messages I have taught. Because I did not feel that I had an answer to the problem, I didn't pursue it. But the more widely I traveled in America and Europe, the more convinced I became that the modern Church is on the same road that Judah took. We know that road took them into Babylonian captivity. We don't need that destination. Thus I accepted the challenge to "sound the alarm!" I wrote the final chapter of this book first and let it sit in the computer for nine months. Convinced that this was God's ultimate answer to an idolatrous heart, I wrote the rest of the book.

If this book opens the eyes of only a handful of saints to the presence of idols among us, it will be worthwhile. We need to heed the warning of the prophet Hosea who wrote, "Because Ephraim has made many altars for sin, they have become for him altars for sinning" (Hosea 8:11).

Judson Cornwall
Phoenix, Arizona
1990

Chapter 1

The Profusion of Altars

Attributed to Benjamin Franklin is the saying that only two things in life are sure: death and taxes. I believe, after having traveled throughout much of the world, I could add a third item to this list: **altars**. I have seen that no matter how ancient the culture, people had and presently have their altars. Archaeological discoveries repeatedly evidence the existence of altars as part of the long story of man's past. Prehistoric cave paintings depict sacrificial acts around an altar. Early hieroglyphics tell of worship at an altar. Carvings in stone pillars, crumbling on archaic temple sites, give examples of altar styles, as well as the garb of priests who served at the altars. It is difficult for us to visualize ancient worship without imagining some form of an altar, for altars are often the only vestige of a religion that has survived the passage of time.

From its beginning, mankind has found it imperative to worship, and altars have been an integral part of that experience. It is not too uncommon, if hiking in certain regions of the United States, to come upon the remains of primordial Indian altars once used in worship. A circular stone heap, sometimes with a large, angular center stone, often signifies such a ritual. Temple ruins with grand altars have become tourist attractions in Mexico because of their religious significance. On mountain peaks throughout Europe, primitive altars of worship still stand after hundreds of years. In fact, I have yet to visit any nation or culture in the world that lacked an altar. It may be a simple crucifix displayed in the front of an humble clay dwelling or the magnificent center of attraction in an ornate temple. Whether the private place of worship for a single family or a public shrine open to the entire populace, some form of an altar will always be seen.

While some altars are so sacrosanct that only a few consecrated persons dare approach them, others are displayed on the corner of a busy street in a major city, openly exposed to believers and nonbelievers alike. In many homes, especially those of ancestral worshipers, a small shelf in the corner of a room becomes an altar; other religious persons hide their altars lest the authorities discover the illegal rites that are performed there.

I have examined massive stone altars so intricately carved as to defy accurate description, and I have knelt at evangelical altars that were crudely constructed benches. I have gazed in amazement at altars made of beaten gold, and I have seen primitive altars made of mud. Some of the altars I have visited were housed in cathedrals that took skilled men decades to build, while others were located in tents and brush arbors erected by common laborers in less than a day. Each altar was a sacred place of homage for the worshipers. Whether they are simple or complex, ornate or ordinary, public or private, altars have consistently been an intricate part of civilization. The march of time and the progress of science has completely outdated much of the ancient cultures, but the altar remains. It doesn't matter if it is the massive and costly altar at the Vatican or a simple dining room chair in a humble farmhouse in North Dakota. Men and women still need a place where they can contact their god. The human spirit needs an altar of worship.

Altars are tools of expression

As we entered into the decade of the nineties, multitudes of people watched their television screens in a near state of shock when Soviet President Mikhail Gorbachev stood before Pope John Paul II in the Vatican and announced that although his communist nation is atheistic, he has come to recognize a spiritual hunger inherent in people that demands expression. He pledged to work toward religious freedom for his people. For over seventy-five years, Russian leaders have sought to prove that there is no god other than the state system, but, like leaders of other cultures before them, they have discovered that the need to worship is built into the nature of mankind. This awareness of the divine — the inner urge to contact a superior force — is a major link that separates humans from the animal world. God created mankind by His expressive hand, and with His energetic breath He gave man life. Since something of God exists in each baby born into this world, that "something" eventually reaches out for contact with the divine Being. Culture, association or training may direct the way an individual reaches toward God, but consciously or subconsciously, he or she will seek to communicate with the Almighty sometime, somewhere and in some way. An altar will facilitate that communication.

Altars are places of revelation

From antiquity, altars have been useful bridges of expression between persons and their deities. They have also been places where God actively revealed

Himself to worshipers. A confrontation between the prophet Elijah and the priests of Baal in First Kings chapter 18 forcefully illustrates such a memorable revelation of God. Elijah proposed a contest between Jehovah and Baal. The issue Elijah raised would produce a revelation of the one true god at an altar erected in his honor. Since Baal was perceived as a fire god, Elijah projected that the god who answered by fire must be worshiped as the true and living god. The priests of Baal built their altar. They offered their sacrifices. All day long, they cried to Baal. But Baal could not be enticed to demonstrate himself in any manner. At the time of the evening sacrifice, Elijah stepped to the fore. He constructed a crude altar of twelve field stones, dug a trench around it, then placed his sacrifice upon it. To preclude any deceit of a hidden coal or flame, he directed that twelve barrels of water be poured over the sacrifice. Elijah prayed a simple prayer of about sixty words asking Jehovah to answer by fire. Fire fell from heaven to consume not only the sacrifice, but also the very stones of the altar. The fire then "licked up the water that was in the trench" (1 Kings 18:38). Recognition of God was immediate by the witnesses, for "... when all the people saw it, they fell on their faces; and they said, 'The LORD, He is God! The LORD, He is God!' " (1 Kings 18:39) It was a turning point in the worship of Israel, and it all hinged upon the action at the altars. Jehovah revealed Himself to be the only true and living God.

That was neither the first nor the last time God used an altar as a place of revelation. Again and again, God revealed Himself to Abraham at an altar. The most notable of those occurrences was on Mount Moriah when Abraham was asked to offer his son Isaac as a sacrifice to God (see Genesis 22:2). We get an early glimpse of Jesus Christ, our substitutionary sacrifice, in that revelation.

Later, God disclosed a different aspect of His nature to Jacob. Genesis chapter 28 describes Jacob's first night on the desert after leaving home to go to Haran in search of a wife. There God revealed Himself in a vision. Jacob saw a ladder reaching from earth to heaven. Angels ascended and descended upon it. Upon awaking, Jacob responded to the presence of God with the erection of a simple altar. He took a stone, subsequently called a masseba, i.e. a "holy stone," and set it up for an altar to commemorate the site of divine revelation. He poured oil upon it and made his vows to God. What a beautiful image the ladder portrays of Jesus — man's access to God — for man. Christ is the divine ladder. In the New Testament, He told Nathanael, "Most assuredly, I say to you, hereafter you shall see heaven open, and the angels of God ascending and descending upon the Son of Man" (John 1:51).

Again and again, Jehovah revealed something of His nature at an altar, or an altar was built to commemorate such a revelation. For instance, when God revealed Himself as the protector of His people in Israel's first confrontation with an enemy after the Red Sea victory over the Egyptians, Moses constructed an altar and named it *Jehovah-Nissi* — "The LORD Is My Banner" (Exodus 17:15). After Gideon was commissioned to deliver Israel from the hand of the Midianites, he built an altar and offered a peace offering. When fire rose out of the rock and consumed the meat and the unleavened bread, the Angel of the LORD departed out of his sight and Gideon called that altar *Jehovah-Shalom* — "The LORD Is Peace" (see Judges 6:24).

Altars often give a visual representation of the deity

Jehovah God expressed Himself at those altars, but most altars are built as an expression of humans toward their gods. Few of us successfully pour out our adoration to an abstract concept. Therefore builders of altars frequently seek to give a visual representation of the god they worship. I have observed the crucifix commonly displayed at altars in Catholic-dominated societies. Altars in Buddhist nations have an idol of Buddha as part of the decor. People given to the worship of demons have many forms of demonic caricatures decorating their altar sites. Most Protestant places of worship settle for symbols such as a cross, an open Bible, a descending dove, a lamb or grape clusters. Although greatly diverse, each form of decoration is an attempt to give expression to the worshipers' concept of God.

In contrast, knowing this need exists in the heart of humanity and understanding that Jehovah cannot be reduced to pictures, engravings or visible symbols, God commanded that His altar be constructed simply and plainly of earth or uncut stones. Even the lavishly decorated Tabernacle in the Wilderness used nothing but bronze-covered boards to hold a mound of earth as the place where sacrifices were to be offered to Jehovah. The beautiful carvings, the work of beaten gold, the tapestries and lavish ornamentation were reserved for the Holy Place and the Most Holy Place in the presence of God. But the outer court, where sin with its penalty and pollution were dealt with, was kept plain and simple. The brazen altar, a type of the cross, was the least glamorous of all the pieces of furniture in the Tabernacle of Moses.

Much later when Solomon built the very ornate Temple in Jerusalem, he enlarged, embellished and multiplied the other pieces of furniture, but the brazen altar was left simple in clear, obedient response to God's plan.

God's altar pictures His provision, not His person

God did not intend His altar to be a representation of Himself. He wished for the altar to be seen as propitiatory, since its purpose was forgiveness of sin through substitutionary death. The Christian altar portrays the cross of Jesus, which had nothing glamorous about it. That cross was an instrument of torture, punishment and death, yet it is God's only answer to sin. While man cannot convince God to overlook sin, man can receive complete pardon for sin by confessing the sin and identifying with the substitutionary death of Christ Jesus at Calvary.

The second of the Ten Commandments says:

You shall not make for yourself any carved image, or any likeness of anything that is in heaven above, or that is in the earth beneath, or that is in the water under the earth; you shall not bow down to them nor serve them (Exodus 20:4-5).

Since God was just beginning to reveal Himself to the inhabitants of the earth, He didn't want people to try to depict their concepts of the Divine. Nor does God want our concepts of Him to be limited by anything we have seen or imagined, "For since the beginning of the world men have not heard nor perceived by the ear, nor has the eye seen any God besides You, who acts for the one who waits for Him" (Isaiah 64:4).

Still, God knows that we learn by proceeding from the known to the unknown, and that our concepts of the abstract are usually extrapolations from the concrete. Paul suggested that God first demonstrates Himself in natural things before doing spiritual things (see 1 Corinthians 15:46). Because we need something to help formulate our concepts of God, the Bible has given us hundreds of similes, symbols and illustrations of God. These range in part from lamb to light, from shepherd to savior. God is seen as a mighty warrior and as a tender lover, but He is also pictured as a vine with branches and as a root out of the dry ground. No one symbol gives a complete concept of God, for as Job declared, "He does great things past finding out ... " (Job 9:10)

Altars reveal the concept of the worshiper

Altars not only give visual portrayal of the god being worshiped, but the very use of the altar also reveals the concept the worshiper has of his or her god. If one envisions his or her god as harsh and vindictive, then that worshiper may feel he or she must placate the deity with costly sacrifices. Even worshipers of Jehovah who see His judgmental nature without comprehending His forgiveness and grace often approach God's altar in an attempt to appease Him. They usually enter into some form of self-flagellation or deprivation, seeking to pacify an angry God. All sensitive altar workers have learned to spot persons with such concepts of a vindictive God. Conversely, if a worshiper has an image of God as gentle and beneficent, the altar may well become a place of offering incense or flowers. Christians who see God as beneficent are more likely to offer song, praise and adoration to God on their altars of worship. Just as it is difficult to praise the patrolman who is issuing you a ticket, so it is perplexing to try to praise God when we envision Him as an enforcer of law.

Even a casual observance of the way an altar is used will reveal much of the attitude the worshiper has of his or her god. Where the god is seen as human in nature, food and drink are offered on the altars, but when the god is considered a super being, costly gifts are presented. Quite universally, worshipers have felt that pain and suffering gain the favor of their god, and thus human sacrifices have been considered the ultimate gift to a deity. I have ached as I watched idol worshipers crawl on their knees across cobblestone courtyards seeking to appease their god. I have felt anger as I watched very poor persons bring money and food to their idols, for I knew that doing so literally took food out of their mouths. I have also felt anguish as I worked around evangelical altars with persons whose concepts of Jehovah God were so low that they could not approach Him in faith, love or rejoicing. Altars are, indeed, tools of expression. The way they are used becomes the language of the soul in worship and quite accurately reflects the concept the worshiper has of his or her god.

Altars are consistent with Scripture

Altars abound in the Scriptures. They became places in which to contact God, communicate with God, and worship Him. They also became places for the propitiation for sin, the offering of gifts, and the making of covenants with God. The altar became the bridge between the human and the divine. It was the place where men and women interacted with God. How legitimate, then, that they were viewed as sacred places.

Altars are mentioned in 25 books of the Old Testament and in 8 books of the New Testament. The ritual of substitutionary sacrifice, which begins in the Garden of Eden, is pictured from Genesis through Revelation. The first record of false worship was when Cain offered the fruit of the ground instead of offering a lamb. Cain was placed under the curse of God for the rest of his life because of his disobedience at the altar (see Genesis 4:3). Conversely, when Noah stepped out of the ark, having escaped God's judgment upon the earth, his first act was to build an altar to the Lord and to offer proper sacrifices on it (see Genesis 8:20). Later Abraham walked as a pilgrim and a stranger in a land into which God led him. He built altars to the Lord virtually everywhere he set up his tent. Abraham's son Isaac continued the great tradition of building altars, as did his grandson Jacob.

Long before the law of Moses was codified, building altars as a means of worship was commonplace because altars helped localize a point of contact with the divine. While the sense was not that God actually inhabited the altar, the altar was a place where the God of all the universe could be reached by earthbound people.

When God gave the law and ordinances of worship to Moses, He specified the use of altars in the worship of Jehovah. The Tabernacle became the place where His altar would continue, and He established a priesthood to assist individuals in their use of the altar. Guesswork was replaced with guidelines, and specific uses of the altar were outlined to help the worshiper in his approach to God.

During the forty years when Israel wandered in the wilderness, life was far more complex than the simple nomadic existence of Abraham, Isaac and Jacob. Individual sacrifices could have intimidated or endangered the society in Israel's massive camp, to say nothing of the sanitation problem it would have created. So God centralized the altar and made its use far more elaborate. None of the former uses of the altar were withdrawn; they were corporately embellished. Jehovah made the site of His altar a very sacred place that was attended by men He chose and sanctified to the position of priests. There any person in the camp could come to present a variety of sacrifices to Jehovah.

God commanded that this centrality of the altar continue when Israel entered the Promised Land. Knowing that the people would be exposed to the places in the land where others worshiped their gods, the Lord commanded the second generation:

> You shall utterly destroy all the places where the nations which you shall dispossess served their gods, on the high mountains and on the hills and under every green tree. ... You shall not worship the LORD your God with such things. But you shall seek the place where the LORD your God

chooses, out of all your tribes, to put His name for His habitation; and there you shall go. There you shall take your burnt offerings, your sacrifices, your tithes, the heave offerings of your hand, your vowed offerings, your freewill offerings, and the firstlings of your herds and flocks. And there you shall eat before the LORD your God, and you shall rejoice in all to which you have put your hand, you and your households, in which the LORD your God has blessed you (Deuteronomy 12:2,4-7).

Israel observed this commandment consistently until after the loss of their priesthood in the death of Eli and his sons. During the leadership of Samuel, sacrifices were offered at various locations suggesting that the loss of the Ark of the Covenant in the battle with the Philistines diminished the sense of the sacredness of the altar. It is not until David returned the Ark to Jerusalem many years later that we again see a central place for God's altar. David so desired to construct the formal sacrificial temple given to Moses that it was reestablished in Jerusalem and it remained there until the city's destruction. Seventy years later when the Jews were allowed to return from Babylon, the rebuilding of the Temple, with its altars, had priority over everything else. When construction was neglected and the people began to lose interest, God inspired prophets to call the people back to their commitment of rebuilding a centralized place of approach to God.

It was an indisputable inconvenience for the Israelites to have to come to Jerusalem to worship, but God commanded:

Three times a year all your males shall appear before the LORD your God in the place which He chooses: at the Feast of Unleavened Bread, at the Feast of Weeks, and at the Feast of Tabernacles;

*and they shall not appear before the LORD
empty-handed* (Deuteronomy 16:16).

Four additional feasts were provided for those who
wanted the option of more worship experiences.

Not until Christ Jesus' ultimate sacrifice on the
cross of Calvary could we understand the vital impor-
tance of a central place for God's altar of propitiation.
The New Testament repeatedly teaches us that Christ
is God's ultimate sacrifice for sin, and that there is no
other accepted approach to God. Christ Jesus is not
only our offering for sin, He is also our place of contact
with God and our channel of communication with Him.
Any other approach to God meets with failure. Jesus
said, "I am the way, the truth, and the life. No one
comes to the Father except through Me" (John 14:6).
None of us is allowed to choose our place of meeting
with God. It must be in Christ Jesus. Neither is an individual allowed to design his own altar. The cross is
God's accepted altar of sacrifice. As Peter declared:
"Nor is there salvation in any other, for there is no
other name under heaven given among men by which
we must be saved" (Acts 4:12).

God's monopoly was exchanged for multiplicity of altars

God carefully guards His altar — its nature, use
and even location — to perpetuate the purity of man's
worship of Jehovah. He maintains a curious jealousy
over it, and categorically rejects all substitute altars.
Since God declared a monopoly on altars of worship,
how does it happen that the prophets consistently
speak of a multiplicity of altars? The answer is quite
simple. These other altars were not erected to Jehovah,
but were altars to idols and heathen deities. So
profuse were the numbers of these altars that God
cried through Jeremiah: "... according to the number
of the streets of Jerusalem you have set up altars to

that shameful thing, altars to burn incense to Baal" (Jeremiah 11:13). They were altars to heathen gods erected in the holy city of Jehovah. Could their profanity have been expressed more vividly? Israel not only worshiped other gods; they did it on Jehovah's territory, and, as Ezekiel saw, even in Jehovah's house.

Worshiping God's way seems so simple to those of us looking back in history. But of the persons who lived the experiences, we merely read how difficult it was to override the inherent human tendencies to appropriate and assimilate surrounding foreign religious influences. Certain rites and motifs attracted the Hebrews. Some of those rituals appealed to their carnal natures. In addition, having an altar on the roof top, or in a grove of trees on one of the rolling hills of the farm, made worship more convenient. But God insisted that He be revered in the place where He had placed His name and in the way He had prescribed. The altar in Jerusalem that was built for the worship of Jehovah was an altar of holiness, while the many other altars scattered throughout the land were altars for sin. God said: "Because Ephraim has made many altars for sin, they have become for him altars for sinning" (Hosea 8:11).

Ours is a far more advanced culture. Although we commonly use knowledge that was totally unheard of in the days of David and the prophets, our human nature remains unchanged. We are just as allured by heathen society as were the Hebrews. Our carnal nature still cries to be satisfied, even if that means violating the commands of God. Although we know God's provisions, like spoiled children we declare, "I'd rather do it my way!" In our attempts to improve God's altar of approach, we often build our own altars for sinning. It seems that the human soul develops a propensity towards altars for sin.

Little children, keep yourselves from idols. Amen
(1 John 5:21).

Chapter 2

The Propensity
Toward Idolatry

A passerby, in glancing through a window to a party taking place inside a house, may observe the revelry, but remain far removed emotionally. While the guests inside release their inner excitement, the person on the outside may be unable to equate his own circumstance or mood with the party atmosphere. Yet if the observer becomes a participant, he might begin to experience the hilarity and join the crowd in their celebration.

Everyone, at one time or another in life, has wished to be more than the person on the outside looking in. But there are places and times, when by conscious choice, I have been glad to remain a spectator on the outside. In witnessing the dire results of excessive drinking, or in viewing the drunken behavior of an alcoholic, I have preferred to abstain from using alcohol. One look at a derelict in a drunk tank should be sufficient to prevent any observer from drinking. Unfortunately, it is not. Viewing the end result of drug abuse should deter the entire populace from experimenting with any and all deadly substances. However, not many have been persuaded that the advantage of the one on the outside looking in far exceeds the emotional high of the one on the inside trying to see out. The attraction of temporary pleasures draws new users into drug abuse — regardless of the permanent penalties and self-destruction.

Although the Bible clearly declares that "… the wages of sin is death" (Romans 6:23), and life around us repeatedly demonstrates this truth, men and women still choose to sin, for there is a power in sin that the Bible calls "the passing [or temporary] pleasures of sin" (Hebrews 11:25). Persons seem to get so caught up in the momentary pleasurable sensations of sin that they ignore its end. They fail to recognize the cause and effect relationship between sin and death. Ignoring it, however, does not prevent its working. Death follows sin as surely as night follows day.

Israel's religion, grounded in revelation rather than in superstition, speculation or philosophical reasoning, sadly degenerated into paganism. I have been a lover of the Old Testament from my boyhood days, and at the writing of this book, I have been preaching for nearly sixty years. Yet no amount of reading, research or pondering has satisfied that unceasing longing to know what it was that so desensitized Israel to such gross idolatry. Perhaps the person on the outside looking in retrospect to the events of history may never fully comprehend the vice, moral degeneracy, political corruption, oppression and idolatry. Ignoring the cause and effect connection between sin and death seems to have been the case for Israel. God's chosen people rebelled against His law, transgressed His covenants and insisted on their own form of government. To legitimize their actions, they made a religion of their rebellion. Israel did not substitute sinning for worship; she made sinning an act of worship. Perhaps to fully enjoy the brief pleasure of sin, it becomes necessary to make a religion of it. Hence, even in the twentieth century, we have "altars for sinning" erected throughout the civilized and primitive world. Having written about Israel's idolatry and God's severe judgment upon those idolaters, Paul penned, "Now all these things happened to them as examples, and they were written for our admonition, on whom the ends of the ages have come ... Therefore, my beloved, flee from idolatry" (1 Corinthians 10:11,14). God faithfully records the perversion of Israel so we can see the pattern that leads to idolatry. Unfortunately, few persons heed the modeled warning. We need to remind ourselves of the words of the sage: "He who will not learn from history is condemned to repeat it himself."

When trying to understand Israel's propensity to idolatry, we need to remind ourselves that the Israelites were not sinners above all sinners. They were a chosen people who lived in the love and grace of God. They had experienced generations of relationship with Jehovah and had participated in a demonstration of His mighty power and love that delivered them out of Egypt and preserved them in the wilderness for forty years. God gave them the law, the Tabernacle, the priesthood and the inspired rituals of worship. When they insisted on having a king like the other nations around them, God gave them a king and, later, even allowed Solomon to build a temple to Jehovah. It was God's pleasure to give them their hearts' desires, and God repeatedly raised up prophets to instruct them in God's desires for them.

They were a very special people. God had said, "Now therefore, if you will indeed obey My voice and keep My covenant, then you shall be a special treasure to Me above all people; for all the earth is Mine. And you shall be to Me a kingdom of priests and a holy nation" (Exodus 19:5-6). God designed them to be a priestly kingdom, but He purposed that all of their priestly activities be directed toward Him. They were to be in His service exclusively. What was it, then, that drew them into the service of the deities of the nations they had been sent to conquer and destroy?

Idolatry originated in Eden

The story of the beginning of the man Adam and his wife Eve is without date or timing in the Bible. Just as entire civilizations rose and fell in the space between two verses in Genesis, a great span of time could have occurred in the few verses between man's creation and his fall. During this season, man and God walked and talked together in a most intimate communion. The tempter entered the scene and suggested that disobedience to God's commands would impart such great knowledge as to make this pair the equivalent to God Himself. Adam and Eve set their wills above the expressed will of God and found themselves separated from the intimate presence of God. They had enthroned their wills upon the altar of personal desire and had inadvertently introduced idolatry to the human race.

Idolatry is principally the response of personal adoration toward something less than Jehovah God, whether that something is self, an object made by ourselves, or a concept we may have embraced. An idol may be metal or mental, carved by man or conceived in the mind; but its outer form is less important than the force it exerts upon our lives. An idol is anything or anyone, including ourselves, that is given the credit for the abilities that only God possesses. How often the prophets condemned Israel for saying that their deliverance, provisions or protection had come from a source other than Jehovah God. Adam desired a source of knowledge other than God and became an idolater who needed the redemption of shed blood.

Unfortunately, Adam's propensity to idolatry passed into the human race faster than the imputed righteousness of a sacrificial offering. Before long, humanity was defiled with godless idolatry. The scriptural account reads:

Then the LORD saw that the wickedness of man was great in the earth, and that every intent of the thoughts of his heart was only evil continually. And the LORD was sorry that He had made man on the earth, and He was grieved in His heart (Genesis 6:5-6).

God's answer to this grief was the flood in which only Noah and his family were spared. God desired to wipe idolatry off the face of the earth by destroying all vestiges of idols and idolaters. Starting anew with the righteous family of Noah, He expected pure worship to prevail. But the incident at the tower of Babel proved differently, and Jehovah dispersed humanity by confounding their language. This scattering spread idolatry throughout the developing world.

Civilization formed far more readily around idolatry than around the worship of Jehovah. The Old Testament deals largely with the Hebrews — that segment of society that embraced the worship of God — while often excluding the detailed accounts of other civilized cultures. If one does not understand this biblical principle of limitation, he or she could mistakenly believe that the ancient world fundamentally worshiped Jehovah. History's evidence is to the contrary.

Abraham was God's third attempt to establish pure worship

The Chaldean empire was one of the earliest nations and cultures of idolatry that rose to prominence. Its culture covers several centuries. Early in its development, a man called Abram lived in its capital city of Ur. God called him and his wife Sarai out of their land to go into a land completely unknown. Abram obeyed, and God blessed him everywhere he went. Whether he was already a worshiper of God, or whether this call pulled him away from idolatry, is not stated in the Bible. All we know is that the people among whom he lived were idolatrous to the core.

God changed this man's name from Abram to Abraham, and made him the father of the Hebrew nation. Of the many outstanding characteristics to be seen in his life of obedience was the complete absence of any taint of idolatry. That pattern carried through into the life of his son and grandson until the grandson, Jacob, went back to Haran to secure a wife for himself. Ending up with the two daughters of Laban as his wives, Jacob remained with his father-in-law for a lengthy season; he then decided to return to his own home and people. Jacob and his family left Haran and in an act unknown to him, Jacob's wife, Rachel, stole her father's idols and took them with her. When Jacob discovered this, he confiscated the idols and buried them, for the concept of worshiping Jehovah exclusively had been thoroughly drilled into him by his father, Isaac.

Because of their nomadic lifestyle, the constant separation from other people probably helped keep the lineage of Abraham out of idolatry. God had called them to come out of relationships with idolatrous persons, and they obeyed that call explicitly. Their commitment was complete, but experience teaches us that God eventually tests all commitments. A lengthy famine succeeded in sending the seventy members of this family into Egypt where they remained for nearly 450 years. Their commitment to the monotheistic worship of Jehovah was severely tested, for they found themselves surrounded by hundreds of idols and thousands of idolaters. Those idolaters insidiously became their masters.

The purity of worship Adam had in the garden was lost when he worshiped at the altar of his own will. His true worship of God didn't even make it into the second generation before it was defiled with idolatry. The purging of the great flood restored men to righteous worship through the family of Noah. But even then, living without idolatry didn't make it beyond the second generation. So idolatrous were the people's hearts that God scattered them at Babel. The choice of Abraham again gave God a strain of persons who worshiped God purely, and that time monotheistic worship lasted beyond the third generation. Unfortunately, however, that generation of people was put to the test in Egypt, and they too became idolaters. What is so attractive about idolatry? What is its power of deception? While they are not all inclusive, I do see at least five ways that idolatry gets a grip on worshipers.

Close association with idolaters breeds idolatry

For all the benefits of urban society, it does have its distinct disadvantages. Iniquitous behavior spreads far more rapidly in a city than in the country. Furthermore, peer pressure can provoke persons into actions beyond their personal preferences. It is always hard to stand alone or to feel that you are going upstream when all others are floating downstream. The product of Abraham's sacrifice in exchanging life in Ur for a pastoral life in Canaan was lost when the fourth generation went into Egypt. They were exposed there to a way of life and forms of worship that had been completely unknown to them. The pressure to conform became increasingly severe as they lived among the Egyptians, first as their guests and finally as their slaves.

The more intimate the association, the greater its potential to breed idolatry. Repeatedly God prohibited intermarriage with the heathen. There was a consistent departure from the worship of God to idol worship when His restrictions were ignored. This is illustrated consistently throughout the Old Testament. Even godly King Solomon, endowed with wealth and wisdom, had his heart turned from serving Jehovah to venerating multiple idols because he married many heathen wives who brought their idolatry with them and insisted upon practicing it in Jerusalem. Solomon built temples to their deities and joined in their idol worship until his heart was completely turned from God.

There is no association in our earthly lives that is as close as the marriage relationship. The Bible declares that in marriage the "two become one." If one of the marriage partners is an idolater, it will greatly influence the other party. This seems to be especially true if the woman is the false worshiper, for worship seems to be more consistent to the nature of women; men tend to follow the lead of the woman. The New Testament commands:

> *Do not be unequally yoked together with un-*
> *believers. For what fellowship has righteousness*
> *with lawlessness? And what communion has light*
> *with darkness? And what accord has Christ with*
> *Belial? Or what part has a believer with an un-*
> *believer? And what agreement has the temple of*
> *God with idols? For you are the temple of the*
> *living God* (2 Corinthians 6:14-16).

Although it is not an inexorable law, close relationships with unbelievers, such as in marriage, most often turn the worshiper of God into an idolater instead of converting the idolater into a worshiper of God.

Not all marriage partners form close friendships, but we do need such a friend. Christians need to be aware, however, of the tremendous influence a close friend can have upon his or her life. The wise man wrote: "Make no friendship with an angry man, and

with a furious man do not go, lest you learn his ways
and set a snare for your soul" (Proverbs 22:24-25). The
principle is that the spirit in the sinning friend becomes infectious to his friends. I have often grieved
over young people who lost their faith in God by forming friendships with persons who had no faith in God.

Recently I listened to the heartbreaking story of a
pastor's teen-aged daughter who formed a friendship
with a rebellious young man at the restaurant where
she worked. Before long his rebellion began to work in
her until she eventually ran away from home and
made shipwreck of her life. All the years of home training were set aside to join this "friend" in his rebellion
against life.

The Bible does not seek to isolate us from all con-
tacts with persons who disbelieve in God, but it does
warn us: "Adulterers and adulteresses! Do you not
know that friendship with the world is enmity with
God? Whoever therefore wants to be a friend of the
world makes himself an enemy of God" (James 4:4). Intimate friendship with the world system or those deeply engrossed in it embodies the strong potential of
departing from the faith.

The commerce of Egypt introduced idolatry

As long as the chosen people of God tended flocks
and lived in tents totally separated from other people,
worship of Jehovah seemed as natural as life to them.
But when the Hebrews began associating with Egyptian commerce, they were introduced to different views
of divine beings. They found themselves surrounded
with hundreds of gods, including many forms of
animal life — especially bulls and calves. When they
became slaves to the Egyptians, the Hebrews' task was
to build the many temples and holy cities that later
dominated the landscape. It is to be expected that their
minds would be filled with the ideas projected by the

supervisors, devotees and priests of those gods when day after day the Hebrews' lives were wrapped up in the business of constructing temples to pagan gods. If the mind has been saturated with filth during the day, it will tend to be impure in the evening. It was difficult to worship Jehovah purely when, from dawn to dusk, their minds were filled with pagan concepts.

So strongly were the Hebrews influenced by the idols of Egypt that when God led them out of the land, they brought many of those idols with them. They knew it was Jehovah who was releasing them from slavery, but they were so completely indoctrinated with the idolatrous beliefs of Egypt that it seemed natural to carry images with them. When they thought they had lost Moses on the mountain while God was giving him the law and the commandments, they quickly reverted to the bull worship of Egypt and constructed the golden calf. It seemed to be the proper thing to do. It had become a part of life for them.

The second generation following the exodus from Egypt was surrounded with the worship of Jehovah for their entire lives. They had never seen the idolatrous worship of the Egyptians, yet they had hardly conquered Canaan when they were involved in idolatry. Those Hebrews had never worked in their lives, beyond tending flocks and gathering manna. When they crossed the Jordan river, the manna ceased and they had to live off the land. None of them had ever been involved in farming, so they turned to the inhabitants of the land to teach them agriculture. They were taught to offer a sacrifice to the goddess of fertility before planting the fields and another sacrifice to the god of reproduction before garnering the harvest. This was not seen as overtly religious, it was just farming. Thus they learned acts of idolatry in their commerce that plagued the nation for many generations.

The same thing could be said for many other aspects of their commercial life. They learned to offer sacrifices to pagan gods before beginning major construction projects, and the assistance of those gods was sought through sacrifice before entering into battles. It was just the way life was lived in the land they inhabited; it was quite natural to do things the way the indigenous people did them. Quite frankly, those Hebrews didn't know another way to function. They continued the worship of Jehovah on the feast days, but idolatrous activities that had been learned from the residents of the land were part of everyday life. Idolatry rarely started as a replacement for the worship of Jehovah. It was usually a supplement to that worship, and it was viewed as a part of everyday living. To this extent then, the culture to which they were exposed sensitized them to practice idolatry.

It is quite self-evident that we Americans learn much idolatry from the culture in which we are reared. We bring our democratic principles into the house of God as though they were God inspired, all the while overlooking the fact that they are replacing the theocracy of the Bible. We finance the work of the Lord with the world's monetary system, giving worldly institutions title deed to properties dedicated to our God. Many prefer the world's code on divorce and remarriage to the Bible's code, and the convenience of abortion is embraced over the scriptural teaching of the sanctity of life. Repeatedly, we allow our culture to override the clear teaching of the Word of God, but we fail to see this as a form of idolatry. It simply seems natural to us.

The culture of Canaan inspired idolatry

To some extent, each of us is a product of the culture into which he or she is born. Our physical, intellectual and emotional lives are affected continuously by our surrounding environment. The cultural standards we absorb affect us. The foods we eat, our family solidarity, our patterns of friendship — all relate directly to cultural backgrounds.

The same is true of music. In every culture, music plays an important role in rites and ceremonies, for music has an emotional content that satisfies certain deeply felt needs. A people's sense of history, their joy and sorrow in life, and their relationship to a deity are revealed by their use of musical materials. Thus, any look at early Hebrew culture must include music's contribution to their society.

Jubal is declared to be "the father of all those who play the harp and flute" (Genesis 4:21). This inventor of musical instrumentation came from the lineage of Cain, not from the godly lineage of Seth. Throughout the years, the development of musical skills has been more prominent in the godless line than in the godly.

The first written music is credited to the Sumerians, a powerful people who began moving into Lower Mesopotamia about 4000 B.C. Their land was known as Sumer and Akkad, then later, as Babylonia. History credits the Sumerians with developing the earliest sophisticated civilization. Interestingly, the Sumerians were idolaters in the extreme. Altogether the total number of deities whose names have been found in the Sumero-Akkadian texts is more than three thousand. It is highly probable that the musical skills the Hebrews used were learned directly, or indirectly, from their Sumerian ancestry. It would be difficult to separate the music from the worship to which the music had been inscribed. Because music so appeals to the carnal nature of people, it is often accepted as a religious experience in its own right. Observe how quickly people in our generation make an idol out of a popular singer or vocal group. This is no new phenomenon. The human heart is the same everywhere. Music charms us to worship, and the musician often becomes the object of that worship.

David, for example, was unique in his use of music, for it always flowed to Jehovah and brought the listeners to worship God rather than David. He introduced a different style of music, and even invented musical instruments with which to play that music in worship to Jehovah. Whether or not he consciously knew that the music of the world tended to bring a person to idolatry, David introduced a drastic change in the musical culture of the Hebrews.

During the years of their servitude in Egypt and their subsequent wandering in the wilderness, the music the Hebrews used came from the Egyptians who, in turn, had received it from the Sumerians. When Moses was descending from Mount Sinai with the Law in his hands, he joined Joshua who had pitched a tent partway up the mountain and had remained there in prayer.

> And when Joshua heard the noise of the people as they shouted, he said to Moses, "There is a noise of war in the camp." But he said: "It is not the voice of those who shout in victory, nor is it the voice of those who cry out in defeat, but the voice of those who sing that I hear" (Exodus 32:17-18).

The music was so definitely Egyptian idol music that Moses knew immediately what was going on in the camp. Quite obviously the music they had learned contributed to their propensity to idolatry. Culture definitely defines concepts.

Not only did the Hebrews learn music from idolatrous musicians, but they also learned their art from the Egyptians, who had depicted hundreds of gods in their art work. The Hebrews had been taught to carve and paint images of those idol gods in the temples they built for their Egyptian taskmasters. Therefore, art and idols went hand in hand in their minds. Every expression of the finer points of culture pointed to idolatry.

To help counter this, God gave the definitive, detailed pattern for constructing the Tabernacle in the Wilderness. His instructions were most explicit. Moses was warned several times to be certain he constructed it according to the pattern that had been given to him on the mountain. God did not want pagan Egyptian art in His Tabernacle, so He defined a different form of expression. He especially anointed Bezaleel of the tribe of Judah and "... filled him with the Spirit of God, in wisdom, in understanding, in knowledge, and in all manner of workmanship, to design artistic works, to work in gold, in silver, in bronze, in cutting jewels for setting, in carving wood, and to work in all manner of workmanship" (Exodus 31:3-5). Although Bezaleel and others were already skilled in Egyptian art, God gave him special ability to do things differently so that it would bring the consciousness of the Hebrews to God, not to idols. God's artistry in the Tabernacle dealt with symbols rather than attempting to define God.

It has been said that many Christians formulate more of their concepts of God from religious art and hymnals than from the Bible. Music and art are powerful teaching aids, and therefore can be powerful tools to induce idolatrous concepts and desires. It seems that they contributed to Israel's sensitivity to idolatry.

Education indoctrinated the Hebrews in idolatry

These same civilized Sumerians from whom Israel learned music also gave the world *cuneiform*, the wedge-shaped form of writing that remained in use for three thousand years. This, plus *hieroglyphics* (picture-writing with sound value), formed the basis of written communication for centuries. It came from idolatrous cultures. Around 1700 B.C., the Canaanites invented the alphabet. Probably in the twelfth or eleventh century B.C., the incoming Israelites took over from their Canaanite/Phoenician neighbors the Proto-Canaannite alphabetic script in which they wrote the Hebrew language. Frank Moore Cross in *Early Alphabetic Scripts* says the invention of the alphabet was indeed "an act of stunning innovation, a simplification of writing which must be called one of the great intellectual achievements of the ancient world."

While I dare not suggest that learning to write with the simplified alphabet made idolaters of Israelites, I do assert that their instructors were heathen worshipers of idols. As many college students will admit, it is not always the subject taught, but how and by whom it is taught, that most influences the student. Satan has long used educational systems to propagate his doctrine of worshiping anything other than Jehovah God.

One cannot help but wonder what kind of literature was available to those who were learning to read and write. Many early writings that have been unearthed by archaeologists seem to be odes to gods and are records of great deeds attributed to those gods. Surely that had some effect upon the minds of the students and may have contributed to the development of a mental propensity toward idolatry. Creating an awareness of idol gods might induce a tolerance for them. Unrestricted tolerance, actually bigotry in reverse, is seen in much modern literature, which succeeds in turning the minds of the readers away from Jehovah God.

Training instilled a disposition to idolatry

God and the prophets clearly declare and denounce that Hebrew mothers taught idolatrous practices to their children. When we realize how little contact those Hebrew children had outside their family circles, it must be assumed that what the parents practiced and taught became the rule of life for the children. They had no access to books, radios, television or world travel. If their world was not much bigger than their family circle and their parents practiced idolatry, it would be considered the normal worship pattern for living.

The children we bring into the world are malleable pieces of clay whose permanent shapes are dependent upon our creative hands. Most of the important things children learn about life and living are learned at home. This is especially true in the matter of worship. What a child sees and experiences in his formative years in the home will usually determine what, who, how or even if he or she worships as an adult. A vast majority of people remain in the same religious faith into which they were born.

We have long used the proverb, "Like father, like son," but the prophets said, "… Like mother, like daughter" (Ezekiel 16:44). As the father teaches the son through example as well as precept, so the mother creates attitudes in the life of her daughter. If idolatry is part of the worship pattern for the parents, it will become the practice of the children. This training, whether conscious or not, so instills idolatry in the minds of the youth that nothing short of a divine miracle can ever completely remove it. The wise man said, "Train up a child in the way he should go, and when he is old he will not depart from it" (Proverbs 22:6). This is true for both righteousness and un-righteousness.

I am not unaware of the workings of demons behind idols, but I can only believe that initially, at least, there was something more natural than supernatural that drew the Hebrews into building altars to lifeless im-ages. Association, commerce, culture, education and training stand out in my mind as powerful contributors to idolatry — both for the Hebrews and for modern society. Perhaps if we better understand the purpose for these altars, we will have a broader understanding of their attraction.

Little children, keep yourselves from idols. Amen (1 John 5:21).

Chapter 3

The Purpose of Altars for Sinning

Solomon declared, "I applied my heart to know, to search and seek out ... the reason of things, to know the wickedness of folly, even of foolishness and madness" (Ecclesiastes 7:25). The most brilliant king felt that there must certainly be a reason for wickedness, foolishness and even madness or else only the irrational would be involved in them. This same principle can be applied to the erection and use of altars to idols. Momentarily bypassing the clear teaching of Scripture that demon forces inhabit idols and are, therefore, able to exert some influence upon the human soul, altars for sinning must serve a purpose in the lives of individuals or there would not be so many persons worshiping at these altars.

Superstition and ignorance may be a few reasons why some persons worship idols, but that cannot be the total answer, for many educated persons are deeply involved in false worship at idol altars. These altars are not found exclusively in the jungles of Africa or South America; they are on American university campuses and in the homes of thousands of professional people. Highly religious persons, some of whom hold offices in recognized Protestant denominations, bow regularly before false altars to worship in one way or another. We've seen the propensity of the human heart to hold tenaciously to something short of God, but having once seen a demonstration of the true and living God, we would expect to find emptiness instead of fulfillment in these altars to false gods. Perhaps the Hebrew slaves who had lived in Egypt for well over 400 years — 300 of those years in servitude — could be excused for idolatry, but the Hebrews that came into the land of Canaan knew neither Egypt nor slavery. They had known forty years under the hand of a loving and beneficent God who revealed Himself to them in myriad ways.

By the time of Solomon, it would seem that there could not possibly exist any need for altars to idols. The nation was prosperous, secure and high ranking in the countries of the earth. The people were well-educated and religiously trained. What inherent need, or what force of rebellion, could have drawn their hearts from the pure worship of Jehovah to the impure worship of various idols? What purpose could these altars possible serve them or us?

Response to mystery is a purpose for altars

What we do not know about life far exceeds what we do know. Seedtime and harvest have to be a mystery to tillers of the soil. Reproduction in animal life is sufficient enigma to cause God to challenge Job, "Do you know the time when the wild mountain goats bear young? Or can you mark when the deer gives birth?" (Job 39:1) Life in the world around us is not only a challenge, it is a riddle. Looking into the clear night skies, David sang, "When I consider Your heavens, the work of Your fingers, the moon and the stars, which You have ordained, what is man that You are mindful of him, and the son of man that You visit him?" (Psalm 8:3-4) He, as we, found the order of nature overwhelming. The thought that the Creator of such wonders was interested in and involved with persons on this small planet called Earth was mind-boggling to him.

In seeking to handle the mystery, people have consistently made a god out of the mysterious. For instance, most cultures of the world have worshiped the sun, moon and stars, giving them deistic names and building altars to them. Lacking an understanding of the wonder and power of these great orbs of light, people ascribed divine powers to them and bowed themselves in worship before altars erected to the heavens.

Not so with David. He had encountered the true and living God and could cry: "By the word of the LORD the heavens were made, and all the host of them by the breath of His mouth" (Psalm 33:6); "For all the gods of the peoples are idols, but the LORD made the heavens" (Psalm 96:5); and, "I will call upon the LORD, who is worthy to be praised" (Psalm 18:3).

In David's life, all mystery led him to Jehovah; but in the lives of many others, the unexplained entices them away from God. While we may condemn the Egyptians for worshiping the Nile River, the Hittites for worshiping the sun, and the Amorites for having a moon goddess, many Americans are not far behind in the way they handle the mystery of life. Many of our altars are to the gods of science. We tend to deify men of learning and use their discoveries as the bible of life. Instead of realizing that God is allowing our generation to discover many of His ways and works, we tend to set God completely aside and worship at the altars of our discoveries.

Many professors in our universities and colleges mock all belief in Almighty God, pointing to the discoveries of science as proof that God does not exist. Unfortunately there was a time when organized religion mocked most scientific discoveries declaring them to be unscriptural. Thinking Christians of our generation realize that the Bible and science are not antagonists. Science is a tool to expand our concept of God. The more works of His we discover, the greater His Person must be. Those who reject a specific Creator find unanswerable questions in creation.

The truth is, man must find a way to respond to the mysterious that surrounds him; but the depraved, sinful heart does not want to respond to the Lord God. Our solution to that intricacy is to deify the mystery and build an altar to the creation instead of to the Creator. This resolution is not new. It was common in Rome in the time of Paul. He wrote:

> *For the wrath of God is revealed from heaven against all ungodliness and unrighteousness of men, who suppress the truth in unrighteousness, because what may be known of God is manifest in them, for God has shown it to them. For since the creation of the world His invisible attributes are clearly seen, being understood by the things that are made, even His eternal power and Godhead, so that they are without excuse, because, although they knew God, they did not glorify Him as God, nor were thankful, but became futile in their thoughts, and their foolish hearts were darkened. Professing to be wise, they became fools ... who exchanged the truth of God for the lie, and worshiped and served the creature rather than the Creator, who is blessed forever. Amen* (Romans 1:18-22,25).

This could have been written in our generation!

Request for provision is a purpose for altars

Mankind's earliest concept of deity images a god as one who fulfills the needs of a worshiper. The god is seen as the source of supply. Whether this cry is a response to harvest and increase or the desperate plea of persons facing famine, it consistently is an appeal to a divine being during times of need. Throughout the many cultures of past and present generations, altars have been erected to gods for provision. Sometimes the deity was seen as the god of fertility or harvest, or as the goddess of reproduction. The rites of worship offered were attempts to involve this god in the pressing needs of the moment. The more desperate the situation, the more costly the oblation offered.

Even in America, seasons of great drought can cause state governors to proclaim a day of prayer — petitioning God for rain. The southern states experienced two years of drought during the mideighties. The situation became sufficiently desperate that the governor of Alabama proclaimed a day of fasting and prayer on a Sunday. On Monday, the draught was broken with a refreshing rain that fell on that one state only.

When all goes well, we seldom have a sense of needing God, but when there is a serious deficiency, we reach beyond ourselves and plead for assistance. Some approach Jehovah according to His provisions and promises, while others choose to plead with idol gods at their altars for sinning.

Jehovah consistently demonstrated His willingness and His ability to meet the needs of His people. The plagues on Egypt, especially those that exempted the Hebrews in the land of Goshen, established once and for all His ability to do whatever He purposed. God's subsequent provision of manna, water and occasional meat for the forty years the Hebrews wandered in the wilderness demonstrated His willingness to give to His people even when they were rebellious and disobedient.

The psalmist said of God, "No good thing will He withhold from those who walk uprightly" (Psalm 84:11), and David testified, "Oh, fear the LORD, you His saints! There is no want to those who fear Him" (Psalm 34:9). After the coming of Christ, Paul wrote, "And my God shall supply all your need according to His riches in glory by Christ Jesus" (Philippians 4:19).

Even though the Bible offers us ample demonstration and declaration of God's availability to meet the needs of our lives, most persons treat this as a last resource. "Try anything but God" is the common attitude. Pride prevents many from calling upon God for help to do what we feel capable of doing for ourselves.

At the heart of worship, in seeking provision at idolatrous altars, lies an unwillingness to "trust in the LORD with all your heart, and lean not on your own understanding" (Proverbs 3:5). Many persons would rather trust insurance companies, banking institutions, government programs and even welfare than trust God. They kneel at the altars of their own provision. They worship the god of commerce and put their complete trust in the "almighty dollar." They praise the money managers and adore their institutions. Their trust is in bonds and securities, and they are willing to worship whatever causes them to increase and be productive. Many who worship at these altars know more about the current stock market report than they know about the Bible. No one doubts the sincerity of their worship. The tragedy is that they are worshiping a god of provision who is false, faulty and frivolous. This god has failed other societies, and he is certainly capable of disappointing this generation of people.

Even persons deeply involved in professional religion find it difficult to trust in God as the provider of their needs. Many pastors have failed to move into the known will of God because of the three "P's" of a pastor's life: paycheck, parsonage and pension. They seem to be convinced that their denomination can take better care of them than God can.

The psalmist wrote, "Happy is he who has the God of Jacob for his help, whose hope is in the LORD his God, who made heaven and earth, the sea, and all that is in them" (Psalm 146:5-6); and, " ... from whence comes my help? My help comes from the LORD, who made heaven and earth" (Psalm 121:1-2). Just as all idols are the work of men's hands, the idol of commerce, too, is manmade. The prophet warned, "They shall be turned back, they shall be greatly ashamed, who trust in carved images, who say to the molded images, 'You are our gods' " (Isaiah 42:17). Worshiping for provision only makes sense if we are worshiping a God who has the resources to make provision for us. The work of our hands will never compare to the work of God's hands. Jehovah is the God who made all things. This puts Him in an unlimited position to assist and aid those who put their trust in Him. Trusting Him for our provision does, however, put us in a position of dependency upon Him. It is the dislike of having to depend upon God that brings humanity to its knees before the false god of provision that was invented for a contemporary society.

Reaching for guidance is a purpose for altars

We each get but one chance at life here on earth. There are so many ways of living, so many different things to do, and so many voices calling to us that we consistently fight confusion. We are completely baffled at times and desperately need someone to show us the way to go or what to do. Sometimes that person is a friend or counselor. Through the centuries, persons have also turned to their gods for guidance.

Repeatedly, we read in the Old Testament of heathen kings seeking guidance from their idol gods. The prophet reported:

> *For the king of Babylon stands at the parting of the road, at the fork of the two roads, to use divination: he shakes the arrows, he consults the images, he looks at the liver. In his right hand is the divination for Jerusalem: to set up battering rams ...* (Ezekiel 21:21-22)

Nebuchadnezzar was the most powerful king of his generation, yet he turned to his idols for guidance. If that was the pattern for kings, it certainly must have been the pattern for lesser persons.

In speaking of Egypt, the Lord said, "I will destroy their counsel, and they will consult the idols and the charmers, the mediums and the sorcerers" (Isaiah 19:3). But to Judah, God said, "Call to Me, and I will answer you, and show you great and mighty things, which you do not know" (Jeremiah 33:3). Joshua established an exemplary pattern of seeking counsel from God before entering into battle, and he never lost a conflict. David followed Joshua's example and learned to inquire of the Lord for direction in times of perplexity and danger. God always directed him carefully and specifically.

It is almost incredulous that persons would seek guidance from carvings and castings; the work of their own hands. Yet I have stood in heathen temples and watched people ask direction from wooden images by casting lots before them after incantations. I cannot forget the look of horror and terror reflected in their faces when they failed to get the answer they desired.

Why should anyone go to an inanimate object to seek guidance? We certainly do not need to seek wisdom and guidance from demons when the all-wise God is available to His people. God inspired His prophet to implore His people:

And when they say to you, "Seek those who are mediums and wizards, who whisper and mutter," should not a people seek their God? Should they seek the dead on behalf of the living? To the law and to the testimony! If they do not speak according to this word, it is because there is no light in them (Isaiah 8:19-20).

None would deny that there are men of great wisdom, but Paul declared, "... the foolishness of God is wiser than men, and the weakness of God is stronger than men" (1 Corinthians 1:25). Since God at His very worst is ultimately superior to man at his very best, why do so many Americans, even Christians, turn to our educational systems for direction rather than seek the counsel of God?

We are the most learned generation in the history of the world, but in many ways we don't know where to go with our lives or what to do with our learning. We need help and guidance that is beyond ourselves. Unfortunately, however, much learning has made us proud and arrogant, and too often we refuse to humble ourselves before Almighty God to seek His counsel and wisdom. We prefer to bow at the false altars of training, learning and experience. Far more Christians frequent the counseling chambers of their churches than the prayer rooms. They would rather ask counsel of a Christian psychologist than of Christ. Is it possible that we prefer the false altar to the true?

Relationship with a higher being is a purpose for altars

From creation until this generation, people have been earthbound. Even though we have placed men on the moon for a brief exploration, have pierced outer space with our rocket-powered probes, and now use telescopes that reach sight areas millions of light years away, humans are still fundamentally confined to this planet. Notwithstanding, there is an upward tug in each of us somewhat akin to the pull of an invisible kite on a string. It matters little what interpretation the mind may give to this tug on the soul, the human spirit wants to respond to it. The eternal part of each person yearns for contact with something or someone beyond the bounds of earth. Through pagan history, as well as across the pages of the Bible, this something or someone is defined as a god. The altars built to worship this concept of a divine being are overt attempts of individuals and groups of persons to enter into a relationship with this god. It is often a desire to become part of the family of the gods — to embrace that god as "father."

Jehovah knew well this abiding instinct in the human spirit, for He created man with this need. To satiate this desire, He repeatedly offered Himself as a Heavenly Father. David declared: "A father of the fatherless, a defender of widows, is God in His holy habitation" (Psalm 68:5), while another psalmist cried: "You are my Father, my God, and the rock of my salvation" (Psalm 89:26). Jesus repeatedly taught the disciples to relate to God as "Father." The New Testament clearly demonstrates the parent/child relationship between God and the worshiper, and this intimacy with Jehovah satisfies a deep need of dependency that is part of our human nature.

To satisfy this need, many persons prefer to build altars to sin rather than respond to Jehovah as their eternal Father. They don't want the responsibility that comes with such a familiar relationship. They choose to relate to para-spiritual experiences induced by drugs, or to sub-spiritual experiences in which they contact demonic powers. They favor committing themselves to anything other than the one true God.

Sometimes people reject Jehovah as their Father because of the extreme differences between the natures.

God is ultimately holy; they are fundamentally unholy, and feel very uneasy in His presence. They would rather relate to a god closer to their level. They prefer a god who is more like themselves, so they worship a deity who is envisioned as degenerate, depraved and defiled. The projected concepts of idol gods picture all this and more. These gods are seen as selfish, sensual and sadistic beings. Rejecting righteousness, these persons relate to an unrighteous god and build altars to sin at which to worship him or her.

At other times, people reject Jehovah as their Father because of the discipline that being His child would bring. As we will see in the next chapter, we tend to become like the object of our worship. To become a loving member of the family of God is to submit to His chastening and control. The Holy Spirit will work within us to make us conformed to the image of God's Son, and many persons do not want this. Preferring to remain just as they are, they seek to form a relationship with someone above or beyond themselves that will not fundamentally change their way of life. They build their altars accordingly.

Recently the pastor of a church where I was ministering told me of a Ph.D. candidate from a local major university who, with his wife, visited one of the services in this church and experienced the presence of God in a most marked measure. When leaving after the service, he told the pastor, "Whew! I've never felt such love, worship and holiness, but I think we need a church a little closer to hell." It was his last visit.

Reaction to convenience is a purpose for altars

As we've already seen, worshiping Jehovah in the Old Testament was not completely convenient. The limitation of one centralized altar was inconvenient enough for the wandering tribes in the wilderness, but they were always encamped around the Tabernacle so no one had far to walk to get to God's altar. However, when the Hebrews entered the Promised Land and settled in a much wider geographic area, it became far more difficult to get to God's altar in the capitol city of Jerusalem. The constant temptation existed to build altars in the local villages as a convenience to the worshipers, or to set up altars in individual homes.

Convenience was the reason Jeroboam gave for setting up golden calves at Bethel and Dan after the split in the kingdom. He told the people it was too bothersome for them to have to go to Jerusalem for worship, so he made worship available in the north and south portions of the new kingdom. He chose the visual image the worshipers would use, Egypt's calf, rather than the symbols God had given through Moses. Jeroboam also arbitrarily chose the places where worship would be accepted instead of having the people worship where God had placed His name — Jerusalem. He also chose the times for the feasts, and they were not the seasons God had prescribed for His people to come before Him in holy convocation. Furthermore, he made priests of common people instead of staying with the Levites. While his underlying purpose may have been political — seeking to keep Israel from returning to Judah for religious festivals — his projected purpose was convenience, and it caught on with the people.

In theory, at least, they were places for the worship of Jehovah, but in fact, they became places of idolatry. In all of Israel's history, those calves were never torn down or disturbed, although altars to Baal were occasionally destroyed. They were erected and approached in the name of Jehovah, but they were obvious substitutes for His provisions — a convenience for the worshiper.

Modern religion has also substituted dates, places, images and personnel for directives given by God in seeking to make worship more convenient for its constituents. While this may have been done in the name of God, it lacks His presence, His provision and His priests. It has neither His name nor His nature on it. It is far more likely that God sees the whole thing as golden calf worship rather than worship of God.

While Judah could boast that they never forsook Jerusalem as the place to worship Jehovah, the prophets regularly condemned the inhabitants of this land for burning incense and presenting baked cakes on their roof tops to the queen of heaven. They worshiped the stars in the convenience of their own homes. Although modern technology has changed the format, we still do much of our worship in our homes. Television antennae have replaced the incense burners on the roof tops, and one of our favorite pastimes is to worship the television celebrities who appear on our television screens.

Some Christians even forsake the assembling of themselves together for worship, preferring to stay home and "worship by television." They sit staring at the pictured images of their "Christian stars" in an almost hypnotic trance and are quick to send these stars the requested "baked cakes" in the form of dollars. These persons claim that they are worshiping. Perhaps they are, but they fail to correctly identify the object of their worship. Both Israel and Judah claimed that they were worshiping Jehovah, but God rejected their worship, for it was not done God's way, with God's appointed personnel, where God had placed His name. It may have been convenient, but it was idolatrous. They had built altars to sin, rather than approach God's altar of sanctification. It appears that twentieth century Christians are doing similarly — often in the name of God.

Reverting to carnality is a purpose for altars

One of the great attractions of idolatry is that it appeals to the carnal nature of people. It glorifies lust, it satiates greed, and it sanctifies sexual perversion. As long as these gods, or at least their priests, get what they want, no change in human behavior is expected. Quite the contrary, for idolatry both sanctifies and simplifies the glorification of human carnality. Temple prostitutes are available for both men and women, and all acts of sexual immorality are justified since everything is done as an act of worship.

This is in distinct contrast to the worship Jehovah demanded. He declares Himself to be a holy God who wants a holy people. He gives explicit commandments regarding the handling of our sex drives and demands honesty in our relationships with one another. God never made provision to bless our sinning. He came to redeem us from our sinful carnality and to return us to a sanctified humanity. At Calvary, He struck the death blow to the dominion of sin and has declared to us: "For sin shall not have dominion over you ..." (Romans 6:14), but this does not negate the need for discipline on the part of the person who has been freed from the power, penalty and presence of sin. We are commanded, "As you therefore have received Christ Jesus the Lord, so walk in Him, rooted and built up in Him and established in the faith, as you have been taught, abounding in it with thanksgiving" (Colossians 2:6-7).

But many persons have made a religion of their carnality. The drug culture has almost become a religion in its own right. Drinkers have their places of assembly where they celebrate the gods and goddesses of sensuality. Sports enthusiasts have built giant cathedrals called sports arenas or stadiums to worship their idols, while reacting in revelry. Even the homosexual community has sought to legitimize its lifestyle by forming its own churches and appointing priests. While we have few carved idols dedicated to sensuality, we present them in full-color magazine pictures and video tapes. Millions of dollars are spent annually on these idols. Sex is such a popular god that it is used in most advertising campaigns to sell everything from automobiles to zippers. Our society worships at the altars of sensuality, but these altars are altars to sin.

Unfortunately, some seek to Christianize this deification of lust. They have sprinkled a few Scripture verses — usually taken out of context — attempting to put God's blessing on the illicit desire to possess things. The priests and priestesses of prosperity have accommodated the greed of human carnal natures by making a religion of attaining wealth and possessions. Little attention is paid to the means used in acquiring this gain, for the teachers seem to project that the end justifies the means. Such theories are very accommodating, but they clearly violate the teachings of Christ Jesus.

Other leaders in religion have glorified sexual gratification. Often the priest and worshiper indulge their sensual natures in violation of their marriage vows, the clear commands of the Word of God, and sometimes of federal law. This is taught and practiced as a demonstration of "love," in which the beautiful teachings of Jesus about loving one another become a distorted permission for unbridled expressions of sensuality — all done in the name of God, and often as acts of worship to God. It goes without saying that such carnality is never accepted by God as worship. God sees these heinous activities as perverted veneration performed at altars for sinning.

Religious sinning is also a purpose for altars

It is likely that as long as we live, we will meet persons who give themselves over to the drives of greed, pride, sensuality and immorality. What is so difficult for Christians to handle is seeing these persons respond to the lower nature as though it were a religion, claiming to be worshiping God while, in fact, they are adoring their carnal selves. Satan has cleverly turned our thoughts inward from the garden of Eden until now. Adam was told by satan* that God's test of obedience in the matter of not eating from the tree of the knowledge of good and evil was preventing complete fulfillment and development of himself. God was wrongly presented as a great penalizer who was withholding information from His creation. Adam exchanged the worship of God for self-worship through gratification of the appetite's desires, and that propensity has come down through the ages to our present generation.

Somehow true worship of God is visualized by many persons as restrictive. While they have an innate drive to worship, there is an equal desire to express all the fundamental drives of their sinful nature. Just as generations before us have done, we combine these two desires by making a religion out of sinning. We develop a religious philosophy that accommodates our driving passions, and then we turn to the Bible for some form of substantiation for that philosophy. Since relatively few Christians are truly familiar with the Bible, it doesn't take a very clever person to put together unrelated texts to prove whatever he or she might have in mind. For instance, some have taken the cry of Paul, "I beseech you therefore, brethren, by the mercies of God, that you present your bodies a living sacrifice ... which is your reasonable service" (Romans 12:1), and have coupled it with the statement of Jesus, "... inasmuch as you did it to one of the least of these My brethren, you did it to Me" (Matthew 25:40), to demand personal service from believers. It may have been as simple as demanding that the pastor's lawn be

---

*   Take note that the name satan is not capitalized. I choose not to acknowledge him, even to the point of violating grammatical rules.

mowed by a deacon, or as serious as teaching women that when she submits her body to the advances of a clergyman who demands sexual pleasure it is as though she were actually having sex with Christ Jesus.

This is not peculiar to our modern society. It is characteristic of the human nature to want to "spiritualize" sensuality. The priestly sons of Eli did. We read: "Now Eli was very old; and he heard everything his sons did to all Israel, and how they lay with the women who assembled at the door of the tabernacle of meeting" (1 Samuel 2:22). In rebuking his sons, Eli said: "No, my sons! For it is not a good report that I hear. You make the Lord's people transgress" (1 Samuel 2:24), thus putting the full blame upon the priests.

Pious sinning is the curse of religion. Somehow we find ourselves turning to substitutes for God in time of need, and when our wants are sufficiently supplied, we comfortably relate to our basic nature instead of the divine nature of God that was made available to us in Christ Jesus. All of this, and more, is declared to be worship of God. Obviously there is a tremendous potency in altars for sinning.

Little children, keep yourselves from idols. Amen (1 John 5:21).

Chapter 4

The Potency of the Things We Adore

Participation in worship is among the great attractions of idolatry. In the worship of Jehovah, the priest acted as a representative for the Israelite, but in the worship of heathen deities, the worshiper performed most of the rituals. Baking the cakes for the queen of heaven was a family project, while the burning of incense to Baal gave the worshipers "hands on" participation that formed a strong identification between the worshiper and the worshiped. This identification by participation accelerated when the worshipers engaged in sexual rites with the male and female temple prostitutes as acts of worship unto the gods. Scientists now say that the portion of the brain that controls our sex drives joins the segment that deals with the mysterious. It is easy for these signals to cross over. How often have religion and sex mingled over the course of history! The passage of Scripture that defines our very bodies as the temple of the Holy Spirit declares that we should "... glorify God in [our] bod[ies] and in [our] spirit[s], which are God's" (1 Corinthians

6:20). It also asks: "Or do you not know that he who is joined to a harlot is one body with her? For 'The two,' He says, 'shall become one flesh' " (1 Corinthians 6:16). There is an affinity in sexual union that produces a strong bonding. The demonic powers behind idolatry know this and they use it efficiently for entrapment.

There was a further linking of persons with gods in idolatry. The great devotees to Baal sacrificed their children by casting them into sacrificial fires of Molech (see Jeremiah 32:35). While some may have participated in this to get rid of unwanted children, many did this to share the fruit of their bodies with their deity. It was the highest sacrifice they could offer. Baal worship taught that part of their lives was forever in the service of the gods.

All the activities surrounding idolatrous worship helped to form a bonding with the heathen gods. This made idol worship potent. It was far more than religious activity. Idolatry produced an attachment that affected the entire life of the worshiper.

It is interesting that many Christian circles today challenge and condemn the use of physical action as an expression of worship. Do we honestly believe that worship by identification is superior to worship by participation? We have become so accustomed to platform worship by the priesthood that any form of bodily participation is immediately condemned. Modern Christians experience expulsion from churches for merely raising hands in worship, though this is very scriptural. Most major denominations have published articles condemning the use of the dance in worship, and very few even tolerate the clapping of hands in a worship service. They instruct us that worship is to be done silently, and that the congregation should be only observers of the platform activity. Still we wonder why church attendance is so low. Is it possible that the demon world is aware that when we use our bodies in worshiping God, it bonds the worshiper to Almighty God? Americans obediently follow the teaching of their religious leaders. They painfully submit to the Sunday morning hour of religious ritual, but they become fervent participants in the cathedral of football, the temple of baseball, or the sacred court of basketball. Recently in a restaurant in Bryan, Ohio, I overheard a man tell his pastor, "If I would spend half as much time reading my Bible as I spend watching basketball, I would be a far better man." After listening to the counsel that pastor shared in the next half hour, I could understand why that man preferred basketball to religion. He was allowed to be an enthusiastic fan at a basketball game, even to the point of emotionally identifying with his team, but I would hazard a guess, based upon the conversation I overheard, that he was only a passive observer in his church.

Worship is inherent to people

Science would have us believe that a glob of protein protoplasm dropped from space to this earth, and by mixing with the oxygen of the atmosphere of earth became a tadpole that grew to a frog that eventually came to land and matured to an ape that learned to stand on its hind legs. This marvelous creature reportedly evolved to where it could think, speak, play a musical instrument, and establish civilization as we know it today. It is incredible to think that men of great learning could expect us to believe this. It takes more faith to believe such nonsense than to accept the biblical story of creation, which teaches that a superior intelligence, Almighty God, specifically created us and everything that we have around us.

The Genesis account of creation assures us that God spoke everything into existence except persons. In creating Adam, God took of His divine substance and combined it with the dirt of the earth. God then breathed His divine life into this creature enabling man to become "a living soul" (Genesis 2:7). This makes men and women uniquely different from any other living creature. People are peculiar and superior to all creation. In a very unparalleled way, they are the zenith of God's creation, and God gave to mankind dominion and authority over the rest of creation. While all of creation submitted to the dominion of men and women, human beings, themselves, became the special enjoyment of God, the Creator. The psalmist understood this, for he wrote, "For the Lord takes pleasure in His people" (Psalm 149:4).

Created into the nature of each person is something that causes him or her to recognize and worship a superior being. Whether this "something" is an inwrought instinct or the effect of tradition descending from the first worshipers through all the tribes of the human family, man is indeed a religious being; **he will worship!** He must worship. Worship is as natural an instinct as hunger or the sex drive.

No explorer has ever discovered a race of persons who did not recognize the existence of a superior being and worship it. They may depict that faith in a variety of ways, but the spirit within them reaches out and up to something unknown and higher, and there is an inward knowing that they are inferior to their god and thus must worship him or her. The sons of Korah wrote a contemplation about this:

> As the deer pants for the water brooks, so pants my soul for You, O God. My soul thirsts for God, for the living God. When shall I come and appear before God? ... Deep calls unto deep at the noise of Your waterfalls (Psalm 42:1-2,7).

In a poetic way, the psalmist is saying that like responds to like. Life consistently proves this to be true. It is interesting how persons under the influence of alcohol can so quickly find others in the same condition in a crowd of people. Similarly, sports fans find instant rapport with other fans of that sport.

Just as soul calls to soul, so spirit calls to spirit. Whether we recognize it or not, God created us in His image. Inherently, then, we have an inner longing for Him. We may not be mentally conscious of this attraction, but that craving in our spirits for God is there. As I have so often said, there is a God-shaped vacuum in every person's spirit. This craving finds satisfaction in worship. That is why we must worship. There is no other option open to us. A person's choice, then, is not whether or not to worship, but who or what will be the object of that worship. It is the only satisfactory consummation of the deep calling of our higher nature. Mortality must reach toward immortality, for the human spirit longs to contact the divine spirit. This is what draws us to worship!

Conforming to Christ is God's goal for worshipers

The clear teaching of Genesis is that God created man in the image of God, whatever that may truly mean. But this book of beginnings also shows us that when sin entered the human race, it marred and defiled that image of special creation. Men and women need radical transfiguration in their spirits and characters to come back to even a semblance of the original creation. The New Testament teaches us that change in the life of a believer is needful, desirable and available. For instance, Paul wrote: "For you were once darkness, but now you are light in the Lord. Walk as children of light" (Ephesians 5:8). That is not only change, it is a change of polarity — from the extreme of no light to becoming full light.

Again, after listing many forms of sin commonly practiced in the city of Corinth, Paul wrote: "And such were some of you. But you were washed, but you were sanctified, but you were justified in the name of the Lord Jesus and by the Spirit of our God" (1 Corinthians 6:11). Those familiar with this New Testament book recognize that being washed, sanctified and justified was not the cause for their change; this is but a definition of the changes made in them. Those experiences were merely steps in the process of reformation. The cause of their conversion was a change in worship patterns. They stopped worshiping the goddess Diana and started to worship Jesus. When they switched the object of their worship to Jehovah, God began to deprogram them from what the worship of Diana had done to them and to reprogram them in the lifestyle the worship of Jehovah would bring.

In our western culture, we have made a change of life a matter of the mind, but God placed the emphasis upon the response of a person's spirit. It is not merely a change of thinking that produces an experience of salvation, although conversion does, of course, involve a change of mind. It is a change of allegiance in our worship patterns that effects the radical change of conversion. In a very vital way, all of us become like the object we worship. That is why it is so essential for us to be worshipers of Jehovah. It is our only hope of returning to the image God intended us to bear in this life.

We cannot think ourselves into radical change any more than a person can simply wish himself or herself to be wealthy. Accordingly, then, we cannot merely educate a person into conversion. Far too many American churches have given persons who are not converted leadership in the church. They have developed a religious mind, but they have not learned to surrender their lives to the Lordship of Jesus Christ through worship. Their degree in theology has not produced a spiritual transformation in them, nor can it.

Yet spiritual transformation is God's goal for each of us. What sin has removed, God has chosen to restore. God's plan of salvation was not merely to rescue mankind from the presence, power and penalty of sin. God desires to reinstate worshipers to the image of the original creation. In his letter to the church in Rome, Paul said of God: "For whom He foreknew, He also predestined to be conformed to the image of His Son, that He might be the firstborn among many brethren" (Romans 8:29). The resurgence of emphasis on the work of the Holy Spirit in the lives of believers during this past decade has centered more on the fruits, gifts and enablings of the Spirit than on His special office work of making us become like Jesus. Everything the Spirit does is refreshing and vital, but we dare not ignore the fact that it is all done to transform us into the likeness of Christ, and this transformation occurs when we worship.

It was in his second letter to the Corinthians that Paul spelled this out conclusively by writing: "But we all, with unveiled face, beholding as in a mirror the glory of the Lord, are being transformed into the same image from glory to glory, just as by the Spirit of the Lord" (2 Corinthians 3:18).

When we take off our masks of pretense and hypocrisy, which is the meaning of "unveiled face," and come into the presence of God in worship, we enter a process of being changed into the image of the One we are worshiping. Although we may behold only the reflected image of God "in a mirror" because of our limited humanity, what we see is sufficient to effect radical changes in us. The purpose of the mirror of the Word of God is not to reveal God to us. We often see only ourselves in our self-centeredness.

This verse tells us at least six things about being transformed into the image of God through worship. First, it says that the work is progressive — "from glory to glory." God does not effect a complete transformation all at once. He is not in a hurry, and we are unable to accept changes too rapidly. Second, we learn that the Spirit imputes this change — "by the Spirit of the Lord." We do not become God; God is absorbed into more and more of our lives. Jehovah doesn't want us to be God imitators. He has provided for us to become Godlike by imputing His nature to us through the indwelling Spirit.

A third thing this verse teaches is that whatever occupies the attention of the worshiper becomes the model of his or her life — we "are changed into the same image." This, as we shall see, is not only a delight for Christians, but it is the damning force of idolatry. The fourth factor in this change limits transformation to those glorious seasons when we are "beholding the glory of the Lord." Change does not come while we are in God's service. Change occurs when we are in His presence beholding His face.

The fifth teaching contained here is that this change lifts us from one characteristic of God's nature to another: "from glory to glory." Some persons have never discovered that God is more than mere love, although He is perfect love. The Bible reveals God to be a very well-rounded individual with unlimited intellect and ability. As we return to His presence in times of worship, we will see God in higher and higher levels of understanding. The level we have attained in God becomes the platform from which greater levels of glory may be viewed and eventually attained. Every level in God is glorious, but no level is absolute. There is always more revelation and transformation to come. The Spirit adjusts the adorer to whatever level of glory he or she can see.

A sixth thing that Paul declares is that this whole transformation process is a work of God's Spirit — "just as by the Spirit of the Lord." As we worship God, the Holy Spirit makes us to become more like God. The change is not instantaneous, and there are no short-cuts. Fortunately, only dropping out of the program can produce failure. All others are given an opportunity to repeat the course.

The worshiper controls the rate of change. Daily sessions produce daily assimilations into the nature of God. Sporadic sessions spawn erratic changes. It is not God's caprice, but man's constancy, that determines the rate of spiritual maturation and transformation. Three factors controlled by the worshiper govern the change in his or her life: First, the object of worship; second, the intensity of worship; and third, the frequency of worship.

All worshipers conform to the object they worship

In a very real sense, what is true of the worshipers of God becomes equally true of the worshipers of idols. Very high among the curses of worshiping at altars for sinning is that the worshiping person takes on the character of the idol he worships. While often contested, this principle operates with the certainty of cause and effect. The difference is that those who worship Jehovah have the assistance of the Holy Spirit to effect the transformations, while idol worshipers seek change in soul power with occasional assistance from demon forces.

Instinctively, worshipers view the character of the object of their worship as the standard of perfection, otherwise they would not have responded to it as "god." Accordingly, they condemn everything in themselves that is unlike their god, and they approve of everything in themselves that is like that god. This motivates them to abandon everything in life that is condemned by the character and precepts of their god. It also causes them to conform to that standard that is approved by their god. Desiring the favor of the object worshiped, and reasoning that it can be obtained only by conformity to the will and character of that object, the worshiper reshapes his or her views and actions accordingly. Consciously, or subconsciously, the deep longing of a worshiper is to become assimilated, or conformed, to the image of the object worshiped.

This principle works whether we believe it or not. Like gravity, many laws work whether we choose to believe or disbelieve them. Because this is inexorable, we should be extremely careful about what or who we allow to become the object of our affections. The object of our attention, emotions and desires inevitably becomes the object of our praise and adoration. This becomes the model toward which we look in forming our lives.

We need not go back into history to prove this principle. Life amply illustrates it. Look at the person who worships at the altar of sensuality. His or her whole way of life is lustful. The mind feeds on sensual thoughts and images. The eyes of that person mirror lust and the mouth speaks lustful words. The altar at which they worship is revealed by the way they dress, the places they frequent, and the entertainment to which they gravitate.

The same cause/effect relationship can be observed in the life of the person who worships at the sinful altar of desire. Obsession with possessions controls all activities. Dominated with covetousness, the worshiper yearns after everything that seems attractive. He, or she, lives under the spell of greed and avarice. There is never enough of anything, for worship at the altar of desire turns the worshiper into a creature of desire.

We can make the same observations of those who worship the god of power. They soon become power hungry, power brokers, or otherwise obsessed with power. No price seems too great to pay to obtain more power over other persons. They often join the military to work their way up into the ranks of officer status, or they enter the political arena to obtain and exercise this power. This is what they worship, and this is what they become. They exhibit their obsession in every role they play in life. They dominate the home as an extreme authoritarian, and they strive to control every life situation they touch. They worship power and have become power-mad in their living.

Worship conformity is demonstrated in idolatry

The character of every nation and tribe throughout the history of civilization has been molded and shaped by the character attributed to their gods. Since people become like the object of their worship, this is to be expected.

The ancient Egyptians clearly depict the insidious influence of the god worshiped upon the worshiper of that god. Those early patrons of the arts and sciences were brute worshipers. They worshiped animals, especially the sacred bull, ram, heifer and goat. Actually, all the plagues God sent upon Egypt were against the gods the Egyptians held as sacred. Historians report — and ancient Egyptian art confirms — that bestiality, the lowest vice to which human nature can descend, was common among those people. The Egyptian sculpture and paintings reveal that the minds of the worshipers reveled in debased, vile and unnatural desires. Their behavior was consistent with their concepts of their gods. What they adored they embraced.

When we look at the Scythians who finally overthrew Rome, we see this principle demonstrated clearly. They visualized their chief deities, *Oden* and *Thor*, as bloodthirsty and cruel hero-kings. The worshipers possessed a horrid delight in reveling in slaughter, mayhem and bloodshed. Since they believed that one of their hero-gods, after massacring much of the human race, destroyed himself, it was considered ignoble to die a natural death. If not killed in battle, suicide guaranteed them a place in the hall of Valhalla (their heaven).

We can see the same transformation occurring in the worshipers of *Venus*. The Greeks called her *Aphrodite,* while the New Testament calls her *Diana.* Literature proclaims her the goddess of love, but as worshiped by the nations of antiquity she was actually a personification of lust. Acts done in her honor would be "X-rated" even in today's society. During Paul's stay in Corinth, the temple prostitutes who were consecrated to the worship of *Venus,* held the position of the most sacred persons in the city. This was the major source of income for the temple of *Venus.*

From the beginning of civilization until today, men have clothed depraved deities with almighty power. Accordingly, those worshipers of those deities became cruel or corrupt or bestial in their affections. The more they worshiped their deities, the more they became like them. Some of the most brilliant men of that period of history have admitted this. *Plato* speaks of the pernicious influence of the conduct attributed to the gods and suggests that such histories should not be rehearsed in public lest they influence the youth to commit the same evil. *Aristotle* advised that statues and paintings of the gods should exclude all indecent scenes, except in the sacred temples that preside over sensuality. *Petronius*' history of the latter years of Rome and Greece furnish evidence that temples were frequented, altars crowned, and prayers offered to the gods, so the worshiper might render nights of unnatural lust agreeable. They prayed that the gods might favor acts of poisoning, and that they might cause robberies and other crimes to prosper.

The way they worshiped influenced the way they lived. What they worshiped became the character of the worshiper. Considering this, God must be deeply angered when we accept something beneath God Himself as the object of our worship. God repeatedly projects Himself as a jealous God who burns as an unquenchable fire. Today's generation would do well to take another look at the nature of Jehovah God. "God is love" (1 John 4:8), and jealousy is the protective force of that love.

To say the main reason God is so angry with idolatry is because He is jealous of our affections is to miss the real point. God is big enough to overlook the actions of children who are simply acting in ignorance. God is jealous over His people because He knows that when we begin to worship the almighty dollar, our nature will become greedy. Far better than we, God knows that if we worship the goddess of lust, who has become such a patron saint in America, we will become sensuous persons who are immoral and depraved in character. He also knows that as we worship at the altar of pride, we become proud creatures: "pride goes before destruction, and a haughty spirit before a fall" (Proverbs 16:18). Also, "when pride comes, then comes shame" (Proverbs 11:2).

Unless there is intervention to change the object of our worship, nothing can change what we are going to become. We are like a computer in many ways. No matter how costly the unit may be, what is entered into it is all that can be taken out of it. "Trash in, is trash out." What we sow into our lives is what we will reap out of our lives. In speaking of persons who "changed the glory of the incorruptible God into an image made like corruptible man — and birds and four-footed beasts and creeping things" (Romans 1:23), Paul said:

> *And even as they did not like to retain God in their knowledge, God gave them over to a debased mind, to do those things which are not fitting; being filled with all unrighteousness, sexual immorality, wickedness, covetousness, maliciousness; full of envy, murder, strife, deceit,*

> *evil-mindedness; they are whisperers, backbiters, haters of God, violent, proud, boasters, inventors of evil things, disobedient to parents, undiscerning, untrustworthy, unloving, unforgiving, unmerciful; who, knowing the righteous judgment of God, that those who practice such things are worthy of death, not only do the same but also approve of those who practice them* (Romans 1:28-32).

Worshiping at altars to sin not only enables a person to practice sin, but it transforms that person into a sinner. He or she becomes what they have chosen to worship.

The Bible clearly supports this principle

The anointed psalmist contrasts Jehovah God with the gods of the nations surrounding Israel by saying, "But our God is in heaven; He does whatever He pleases. Their idols are silver and gold, the work of men's hands" (Psalm 115:3-4). He describes these crafted idols as having mouths that do not speak, eyes that cannot see, ears that cannot hear, and so forth. They are lifeless figures that depict a human concept of a deity deemed worthy of worship. The Holy Spirit concludes this description by saying, "Those who make them are like them; so is everyone who trusts in them" (Psalm 115:8).

Here is a clear biblical declaration that whenever a person projects the attributes of deity to his or her creation and then worships it, he or she risks becoming exactly like that creation. This is true whether that deity be a visible idol, an ancient myth or a mental concept. In all cases, the worshiper has formed something of his image or likeness, for we can't worship any higher than our concept of our deity. Unfortunately, however, our character easily descends to the level of our concept of deity.

If these altars merely reflected the character of the worshiper it would be bad enough; but altars to idols degrade the character of the worshipers from higher planes to lower. The history of Israel painfully portrays this. When that nation traded the image of Almighty God for the image of Baal, the people degenerated from persons holy unto God to persons unholy in thought, word and deed.

Little children, keep yourselves from idols. Amen (1 John 5:21).

Chapter 5

Israel's Pattern for Idolatry

No nation has ever experienced a greater covenant relationship with God than Israel. Jehovah sovereignly chose this people in Abraham and promised to make them a nation through Isaac. He propagated them through Jacob, protected them through Joseph, and emancipated them through Moses. By sovereign choice, they became the family of God. This positive relationship between God and Israel was so evident that when the queen of Sheba visited King Solomon, she testified:

> Blessed be the LORD your God, who delighted in you, setting you on His throne to be king for the LORD your God! Because your God has loved Israel, to establish them forever, therefore He made you king over them, to do justice and righteousness (2 Chronicles 9:8).

God sovereignly extended a paternal care over His people. He consistently called them "My people" and named Himself as "your God." God led them, fed them, taught them, sought them and brought them to Canaan. He gave them law, religion and a priesthood and sent them an abundance of prophets. He gave them deliverers and judges and miraculously protected them from their enemies.

God sealed His relationship with Israel in a covenant and thoroughly explained it in the law and statutes given to Moses on the mountain. Jehovah also illustrated His desired relationship with Israel in the imagery of a marriage relationship. Hosea, the minor prophet, became a demonstration of this in his life and in his writings. Furthermore, God repeatedly referred to His relationship with Israel as being a husband/wife relationship. God bound Himself to Israel in a two party covenant. It was "I will, if you will." God consistently fulfilled His part of the covenant, but Israel just as consistently abandoned her commitments. Through Hosea, God said: "They set up kings, but not by Me; they made princes, and I did not acknowledge it. From their silver and gold they made idols for themselves — that they might be cut off" (Hosea 8:4). This was strange behavior for a people God declared to be His wife. As surely as Hosea's wife forsook him to run after other lovers, Israel progressively departed from the providential care of Jehovah God. The story of this departure unfolds in the historic books of the Bible, and the prophets plead against it in their writings.

Israel's progression into idolatry

The author of Second Kings masterfully condenses this departure into sixteen verses in chapter 17 of the book. His first statement is as follows:

> *For so it was that the children of Israel had sinned against the LORD their God, who had brought them up out of the land of Egypt, from under the hand of Pharaoh king of Egypt; and they had feared other gods* (2 Kings 17:7).

The writer is neither skipping nor ignoring the years this statement spans. The former slaves carried symbols of the goddess of heaven with them as early as the exodus from Egypt. Because they had idolatry in their hearts, they displayed a strong propensity to idolatry in insisting that Aaron mold the golden calf as a visible object of worship while Moses was on Sinai receiving the Law written by the finger of God. Obviously, Israel abandoned Egypt but did not completely abandon the idolatry they learned in that land. While espousing the worship of Jehovah, who delivered them from Egyptian slavery, they continued to embrace faith in idol gods. They discovered, as do we, that old habits are difficult to break, even in the midst of supernatural demonstrations of Almighty God. Even today, redeemed persons bring much of their idolatry with them as they step from the world into the Church. Many of us find it easier to rename old patterns, habits and actions than to replace them. In stating that Israel "feared other gods," the inspired writer does not charge Israel with abandonment of Jehovah. Departure from God seldom begins as a total abandonment. It is a mixture. Like the Philistines who placed the Ark of the Covenant in the house of Dagon, we add God to our private house of gods. Israel was very dependent upon Jehovah. Initial abandonment would have been suicidal for that nation wandering in the desert eating divinely supplied manna and drinking the water of God's provision. Even after they entered the Promised Land, their only hope of conquest and settlement lay in the providential hand of Jehovah-Jireh. They were in a state of dependency, not of departure.

Their problem was their inability to trust Jehovah completely in every circumstance and for everything. They, as we, also "feared [revered, worshiped] other gods" (see 2 Kings 17:7). They brought some of those gods with them from their former lives. They met most of them as they conquered the nations who inhabited the land that God had given to them through Abraham. There was never a national day when Israel voted to replace Jehovah with Baal, just as there is seldom a one-time act when we exchange a walk with God for allegiance to an earthly idol. Departure from God rarely begins as rebellious abandonment. It usually has its beginning as a mixture. We add other gods to our temple of worship. These subsequently divert, desecrate and diminish the authority of Jehovah in our lives.

The life of King Solomon graphically illustrates this principle. During the construction and dedication of the great Temple, he was completely devoted to Jehovah. Yet as he continued to marry foreign princesses and build places of worship to their gods, he found himself joining his wives in their worship until his heart became so diluted and desecrated that it totally divested him of his obedient service to Jehovah. His example helps us understand Paul's plea in Galatians 5:7: "You ran well. Who hindered you from obeying the truth?" It was the idolatry introduced by Solomon's wives that hindered him. Idolatry introduced from any source will prevent a Christian from running well in obeying the truth of God. That to which we give our hearts soon becomes the controlling force in our lives, for Jesus warned us, "Where your treasure is, there your heart will be also" (Matthew 6:21).

Idolatry is not always as overtly introduced as in Solomon's experience. Long before Solomon, as Israel successfully conquered the land of their inheritance over which Solomon eventually reigned, it became obvious that the conquerors would have to live off the land, for the divine supply of manna ceased the very day they crossed the Jordan river. The early years of conquest were not too difficult, for the soldiers survived sumptuously off the spoils of war, but when they had conquered as much of the land as they felt they needed, they had to learn farming in order to survive.

The first progression was a *learned experience*

It was a new way of living for the generation of Hebrews who had not previously known labor. The slaves who had made bricks, constructed temples, and built cities under Egyptian conscription had died in the wilderness. These warriors were the second generation, who knew only to gather manna in the morning and lead their cattle to the water God generously supplied. Under Joshua they had learned the skills of war, but they knew nothing of farming, tending vineyards or maintaining orchards.

This change in lifestyle was a learned experience as the Hebrews studied agriculture under the tutorage of the undestroyed inhabitants of Canaan. Although they had learned to get full directions for battle from God, they never consulted Him about tilling the fields. Instead, they assumed that the way the local residents farmed was correct. They allowed the enemies of God to become instructors to the family of God, much as today's Church turns to the world to learn the skills of educating, counseling, business management and fund raising.

Somehow it didn't seem strange to the Israelites that the planting of seed was connected with the worship of Ashtoreth (the goddess of fertility), or that the harvest was inexorably involved with the worship of Baal (the sun god). They did not see it as idolatry, for they had learned it as a part of farming. Israel did not initially exchange the worship of Jehovah for the worship of Baal. They merely added those instructions to the divine provision of the festival of harvest (or ingathering). All that mattered to them was that the methods worked. The fields were yielding abundant harvests. To them, the end justified the means. After forty years of living lives completely dependent upon Jehovah, they had begun to divide life into the secular and the sacred. Little by little, they excluded Jehovah from their secular pursuits and reserved Him for the occasional sacred activities of life, which, for them, were compulsory no more than three times a year.

From our perspective of hindsight, it is easy to criticize them for this, but the pointed finger of condemnation ignores the three fingers we direct at ourselves. So much of our lives, and even our church functions, are so secular that they are indistinguishable from the world. We study under the world's tutors, we interact with the world, and we function just as they function. We have our Christmas and Easter times of great pomp and ceremony, but for the rest of the year it is pretty much "business as usual." We have not "come out from the world to be separate" (see 2 Corinthians 6:17); we have gone into the world to be "successful." By the standards of our instructors, many have indeed become very successful; but with it they have equally become very secular and idolatrous. They have replaced their love for the Lord with a love for the world, and they ignore the clear commands of God when they conflict with the teaching of our "canaanite" instructors.

When Christians learn to function in life by observing or being taught by the present world system, we end up with dual philosophies of life. We memorize divine precepts, but we practice worldly principles. We quote: "When in Rome, do as the Romans do" or "You have to play by their rules," even when those deeds conflict with the clear declarations of the Word of God. Little wonder, then, that we function with such a mixture in our lives. Like Israel, we are consciously adding the worship of Baal and Ashtoreth to our secular pursuits while striving to have short seasons when we worship Jesus with all our hearts. It is the beginning of a process that will potentially lead to complete idolatry. It did for Israel. It will for us as well.

This surrender to the ways of the world is insidious, and gains authority in our lives slowly. Even without realizing it, we "fear" the gods of the land. For instance, since democracy is a preferred form of government for us, we like to bring it into the operation of the local church. We feel the majority opinion should prevail, and at least a two-third's majority should rule. The problem we run into, however, is that God considers Himself to be the head of the Church. It does not seem to occur to God that His Church should be governed by the majority vote of the people in that Church. Israel's real problems began when the people voted to have a king as their ruler, thereby replacing the theocratic leadership that God had demonstrated under Samuel. Their explanation was that they wanted to be like the nations that surrounded them. They totally forgot that those "other nations" were the people God had commissioned them to subdue and replace. God's goal was for them to conquer, not copy, those nations. Still, God let them have their way, no matter how rough it became. And sometimes He still does!

Anyone with even a casual knowledge of idolatry knows that it consistently connects sensuality with its worship. That was open and obvious in the days of Israel, for the worship of Baal and Ashtoreth was intricately involved with sexual immorality. Both male and female prostitutes were available to assist the worshipers of those Canaanite deities. Israel found this form of worship pleasant to the flesh and a welcome change from the holiness that Jehovah required in His worship. And so do we. If it was not pleasant, the world wouldn't be doing it, for the unconverted person usually lives for pleasure. Rational people do not deliberately inflict pain on themselves. The things that they do are for the gratification that it produces in them. The result of that action may produce pain, but the beginning is pleasure. No drug addict deliberately started on drugs to become addicted. Initially there has to be a pleasure kick, or he wouldn't try it. Similarly, there has to be gratification in idolatry, or none of us would get involved in it. Unfortunately the initial thrill turns to torment in the end, for it will inevitably lead to separation from God.

The second progression was *walking in heathen statutes*

Israel not only "feared other gods," but they "... walked in the statutes of the nations whom the Lord had cast out ..." (2 Kings 17:8) Not only had the worship of the other nations become attractive, but their ways had become appealing as well. Israel still *worshiped* in the statutes of Jehovah, but they *walked* in the statutes of the surrounding nations. They began to make a distinction between religious and civil law, for commerce and social exchange seemed easier when they adapted to the laws of the surrounding nations.

This distinction is increasingly obvious in our western cultures. Years ago when I was much younger, I received a summons to jury duty. This required me to appear everyday for a full month as a potential juror for trial cases. Day after day, lawyers preparing to try a case questioned me, but no matter what answers I gave, they dismissed me "without cause." Frustrated, I approached a judge and asked why they consistently rejected me from jury duty, even though the county had summoned me to be available. His answer was straight forward. "Don't you know?" he asked. "As a member of the clergy you have spent your entire life dealing with moral law. There isn't a lawyer in this county who wants to trust you with statute law. You see, we aren't dealing with right or wrong, but with *legal* or *illegal*, and we question whether you could make the differentiation."

Sometimes it seems that Christians have almost given up dealing with right or wrong — preferring to borrow the world's idea of legal or illegal. Very often it ceases to be a case of morality and becomes a case of accountability. If we can get by with it in the eyes of the law, we will do it. Like Israel, we "walk in the statutes of the nations."

It is always a big step toward idolatry when the Church abandons God's law to embrace the law of the nations. For example, one in five couples in Sweden live together without getting married. Over half of those living together between the ages of 20 and 30 are unmarried. In that country, raising children outside the bonds of marriage is not only accepted, but the state subsidizes it. Christian leaders in Sweden have told me that this has produced an almost insurmountable problem. Christians don't feel the necessity of marriage, and quickly point out that this is superior to the divorce rate of America. Since the state says it is legal, they don't care what God's Word says.

Similarly, in *America* pre-marital sex is so accepted that ministers among the "singles" find themselves completely frustrated. Furthermore, the civil statutes on divorce and remarriage are quickly replacing God's statutes among the American saints. Christians take Christians to court without any sense of having violated the laws of God. How easily we "walk in the statutes of the nations" and forget that God views this as a manifestation of idolatry.

The third progression was *secret sinning*

Israel's idolatrous practices continued to progress, for we have no record of sin regressing. Sin, like a seed planted in fertile soil, enlarges, matures and bears its hideous fruit. Whenever a person or collective group of persons chooses a substitute for Almighty God, the initial satisfaction soon proves to be temporary, and something must be added to obtain the initial level of pleasure and satisfaction. Sin never satisfies. It always craves something more. Whatever hope idolatry may offer, it can never fulfill a person's life. It is necessary, therefore, to either abandon idol worship or intensify it. Israel chose to escalate their involvement with Baal, but those new acts were in such violation of God's covenant that they sought to keep God from knowing what they were doing.

The historian says, "the children of Israel secretly did against the LORD their God things that were not right" (2 Kings 17:9). Perhaps they assumed God did not observe them because He did not immediately rebuke them. Eliphaz the Temanite asked Job: "And you say, 'What does God know? Can He judge through the deep darkness? Thick clouds cover Him, so that He cannot see, and He walks above the circle of heaven' " (Job 22:13-14). Much later the psalmist reported, "And they say, 'How does God know? And is there knowledge in the Most High?' " (Psalm 73:11) Every child soon learns that the silence of a parent should not be equated with ignorance. Parents, as well as God, often hold back on correction in hopes that the errant child will correct himself. Frequently, however, the errant person accepts silence as either approval or obliviousness. That was Israel's attitude, and it is too often the attitude of modern Christians.

From the consistent revelations in the news media, this attitude is creeping into the spirits of many current religious leaders. Apparently they feel that God doesn't see, so God doesn't care. Their immoral and illegal actions shock sensitive Christians and delight the skeptics of the world. Their behavior has destroyed some, wounded many, and, as Billy Graham was quoted as saying, "... has set world evangelism back fifty years." Only those who are serving the same idols of lust and greed have found pleasure in their behavior. Christians who are secretly worshiping idols besides Jesus Christ have found shelter in knowing there are other closet idolaters in high places.

We need to relearn that God's silence is not synonymous with His approval. He does not forever treat us as little children. When we are mature enough to know right from wrong, He allows us to choose between them, just as He did with Adam and Eve in the Garden of Eden.

Surely we must know that nothing escapes God's knowledge. He is omnipresent (everywhere present) and omniscient (possessing all knowledge). Not only can we not hide our deeds from Him, we are equally unable to hide our thoughts from Him. Job's answer to Eliphaz's statement that God cannot see through the deep darkness was: "He [God] gives them security, and they rely on it; yet His eyes are on their ways" (Job 24:23). David testified: "The LORD is in His holy temple, the Lord's throne is in heaven; His eyes behold, His eyelids test the sons of men" (Psalm 11:4).

Israel thought God had not seen her actions, that none of the holy ones had reported it to Him. Yet God declared:

I know Ephraim, and Israel is not hidden from Me; for now, O Ephraim, you commit harlotry; Israel is defiled. They do not direct their deeds toward turning to their God, for the spirit of harlotry is in their midst, and they do not know the LORD (Hosea 5:3-4).

It was not God who did not know their deeds, it was the perpetrators of those deeds who did not know their God. It is dangerous self-deception to think that anything can be done in secret. All idolatry has its roots in such deception. "Secret" wrongdoing is another step toward open idolatry.

The fourth progression was *misplaced worship*

Israel's fourth step into idolatry is described as: "They set up for themselves sacred pillars and wooden images on every high hill and under every green tree" (2 Kings 17:10). They constructed altars for worship wherever it was convenient for them.

World travelers have observed the presence of temples, mosques, churches, chapels and shrines on the highest geographic elevation in the area. Even the psalmist wrote: "I will lift up my eyes to the hills — from whence comes my help? My help comes from the Lord, Who made heaven and earth" (Psalm 121:1-2). There is something in the spirit of man that chooses to place his or her deity on a high plane, and therefore the places dedicated to the worship of that deity are hilltops, mountain peaks or elevated structures. Even in private homes, idols usually occupy an elevated position in the room.

Since God, the Creator, understood this propensity in humanity, He established a *place* for His people to worship Him. They had the portable Tabernacle of Moses in the wilderness, and in the land of their possession, they had the city of Jerusalem with Solomon's Temple. God insisted that the people worship where He had placed His name. He told Israel through Moses:

> *Take heed to yourself that you do not offer your burnt offerings in every place that you see; but in the place which the LORD chooses, in one of your tribes, there you shall offer your burnt offerings, and there you shall do all that I command you* (Deuteronomy 12:13-14).

When the nation split under King Rehoboam, the ten northern tribes under the leadership of Jeroboam found it was inconvenient and politically dangerous to return to Jerusalem for worship. The new king felt it imperative to maintain separation, so he appointed

Bethel and Dan as the "sacred" cities of the new nation and constructed golden calves as the visible image of the god they served. Those gods were a replacement for the Temple in Jerusalem. King Jeroboam declared it was done as a "convenience" for the people. To further aid in the convenience of worship, Jeroboam appointed the office to almost anyone who desired to be a priest. Whether they were of the tribe of Levi or the family of Aaron didn't matter.

When a leader substitutes convenience for compliance to the Word of God, it is not long before the followers extend that convenience even further. Reasoning that Jerusalem was too far to travel for worship, they soon deduced that both Dan and Bethel (the extreme northern and southern cities of Israel) were equally inconvenient. They soon built altars of worship wherever there was an elevated spot or a convenient grove of trees. There was no sense of the divine presence, just the immediate accessibility of an altar.

Unfortunately, since the human heart is the same everywhere, modern Christians are just as given to demanding a religion of convenience. We want it brought into our homes by way of "Christian TV." We want short, early services that will not interfere with our recreational schedules for the day. We wear lapel pins, display bumper stickers, and support Christian broadcasting, but we consistently forsake the assembling of ourselves together for worship. Many Christians attend a church out of tradition, even if it lacks the presence of God, rather than make the effort to find and attend a place of worship where God has placed His name. We, like Israel, "burn incense on all the high places." We prefer idol worship over worship of Jehovah God if it proves to be more convenient, and it usually does.

The fifth progression was *serving idols*

The chronicler says simply: "... for they served idols, of which the LORD had said to them, 'You shall not do this thing' " (2 Kings 17:12). There was nothing subtle about their actions at that stage. Israel was in open rebellion against Jehovah. They had moved beyond naive accommodation or even merely adding a little idolatry to their worship of God. It may have begun during the days when they were learning to farm, but they had progressed far beyond merely respecting the local gods of the land. God's covenant people were actually *serving* those idols. Israel had exchanged Jehovah for the false gods of the land to live, function and worship as the people around them.

That this broke the heart of God is clearly unveiled by the prophet Hosea when he wrote:

> *When Israel was a child, I loved him, and out of Egypt I called My son. As they called them, so they went from them; they sacrificed to the Baals, and burned incense to carved images. I taught Ephraim to walk, taking them by their arms; but they did not know that I healed them. I drew them with gentle cords, with bands of love, and I was to them as those who take the yoke from their neck. I stooped and fed them ... How can I give you up, Ephraim? How can I hand you over, Israel? How can I make you like Admah? How can I set you like Zeboiim? My heart churns within Me; My sympathy is stirred. I will not execute the fierceness of My anger; I will not again destroy Ephraim. For I am God, and not man, the Holy One in your midst; and I will not come with terror* (Hosea 11:1-4,8-9).

The entire theme of the book of Hosea likens Israel to an unfaithful wife who repeatedly forsakes her husband for false lovers. As an example to Israel, God commanded this prophet to marry a prostitute and try to teach her faithfulness as a wife. Repeatedly, Gomer broke Hosea's heart by her adulterous behavior. Although he bought her back repeatedly, she quickly forsook him for another man.

Do any of us understand the tender compassion God extends in calling us back to Himself without penalty? Neither does God understand how we can abandon such unqualified love for a short-term fling with idols of the world. Perhaps if we understood the love of God, we would never abandon Him for an idol. Even the great apostle Paul cried: "Oh, the depth of the riches both of the wisdom and knowledge of God! How unsearchable are His judgments and His ways past finding out!" (Romans 11:33) Because God is so far above us, we often feel more comfortable relating to something closer to us. It is worth noting that most idol representations are animals over which God originally gave us dominion, or demons over which Christ gave the Church absolute dominion. Somehow we prefer to worship something we feel we can control rather than God who has complete control over us.

Modern religion has used God, abused Him and often abandoned Him for other lovers. It is as though God sits in the heavens weeping as He recounts what He has done for us, while we tell God that we have matured so much we don't need Him anymore. We quickly trade our covenant pledges for more immediate pleasures. We want the thrill more than we want the long-term relationship.

The sixth progression was *refusing to listen to God*

When Israel set her heart upon serving idols, she also closed her ears to hearing from God. The LORD faithfully sent messengers to warn Israel. The passage we are examining says:

> *Yet the LORD testified against Israel and against Judah, by all of His prophets, namely every seer, saying, "Turn from your evil ways, and keep My commandments and My statutes, according to all the law which I commanded your fathers, and*

which I sent to you by My servants the prophets" (2 Kings 17:13).

Israel stoned, imprisoned or threatened the prophets God sent to them. God worked miracles among them, but they failed to see God in any of them. God chastened them, but they refused to hear Him.

God did not cease speaking; Israel simply stopped listening. The next verse affirms this: "Nevertheless they would not hear, but stiffened their necks, like the necks of their fathers, who did not believe in the LORD their God" (2 Kings 17:14).

Many years ago when I was a young father, I took our three daughters to the park to give my wife a brief rest. Dottie, who was five at the time, had the hand of her little sister, and I was carrying the baby in my arms. Dottie saw the swings and started running ahead of me. I didn't want her to get too far ahead of me, so I called, "Dottie, wait for Daddy."

About that time, she stumbled and fell, dragging her sister to the ground with her. They got up, brushed themselves and ran to the swings. When I got to them, before I could say a word, Dottie looked at me and said, "Daddy, I didn't hear you call me when I fell down back there."

When God's people go deaf to His prophets, signs, wonders and chastening, what is left for God to do? Through the prophet, God said:

But you are those who forsake the LORD, who forget My holy mountain, who prepare a table for Gad, and who furnish a drink offering for Meni. Therefore I will number you for the sword, and you shall all bow down to the slaughter; because, when I called, you did not answer; when I spoke, you did not hear, but did evil before My eyes, and chose that in which I do not delight (Isaiah 65:11-12).

Deliberate deafness to the voice of God leads to divine judgment.

A short time ago, I ministered to a congregation in Northern Ireland. Just before my arrival, the pastor had confronted a sinning couple in his congregation. "Do you realize what this will lead to?" he asked.

"Yes, we will go to hell," was their answer.

"Is it worth it?" the pastor asked.

"Yes," they replied.

That was Israel's attitude toward God. The people had determined to build altars for sinning, and nothing God could say was going to deter them. No amount of divine correction could get them to submit. Stubborn, set in their ways and determined to do evil, they stiffened their necks, closed their ears, and continued to worship at their idol altars. They left God few options.

This deliberate deafness to the voice of God is prevalent in today's churches. Repeatedly, I've seen groups of Christians ignore what the Word says and resist what a servant of God tries to bring to them. Declaring, "We have our rights!" they stiffen their necks, walk out, quit the church and often start their own church, which rarely survives more than a year or so. It leaves a group of bruised, bleeding, disillusioned people scattered throughout the area who ask, "What happened?" Stiffened necks and deafened ears brought them to spiritual destruction. Whether knowingly or unknowingly, they had built altars for sinning by insisting upon their way over the ways of God.

None of us "falls" into idolatry. We walk into it. It is a progression that involves flirtation, familiarity and sampling. The more we invest in building altars for sinning, the less we invest in building altars for worshiping God. Time, energy and finances will be invested in one or the other, but when we begin to investigate the world's idols, we progressively tend to shift all energies into the world's altars. Once we have joined the world at her altars for sinning, we quickly learn how to worship idols proficiently, no matter how perverse it may be in the sight of God.

Little children, keep yourselves from idols. Amen (1 John 5:21).

Chapter 6

The Progression of Israel's Altars for Sinning

Sin is cumulative. That is part of its perversity. The smallest sin leaves a residue even after it is forsaken. Although God declares: "The wages of sin is death" (Romans 6:23), He rarely enforces that penalty quickly. God's grace withholds immediate judgment since the vicarious death of Jesus Christ has satisfied God's righteousness. God's delay in sentencing sinners is evidence of His anticipation of repentance. If, however, sinning persons do not repent, they will inevitably repeat that sin with cumulative results. The terrible fear of sinning abates as they discover that God did not immediately impose the penalty for sin. Second, there comes a familiarity with sin, and third, sinning persons come under the tremendous power of sin. While initially they were but samplers of sin, they soon become slaves of sin, for the Word declares:

Do you not know that to whom you present your-selves slaves to obey, you are that one's slaves

whom you obey, whether of sin to death, or of
obedience to righteousness? (Romans 6:16)

This perverse build-up of sin from temptation to tyranny is, of course, gradual. Free people seldom submit to captivity in one quick action. They relinquish their freedom little by little until those who once ruled become the servants. Similarly, sin exerts its controlling power over the lives of participants very slowly; but every surrender becomes a deposit to the account of sin. The day comes when sin takes control over the life of the sinner and the sinner loses his control. Slavery begins at that point.

Isaiah illustrated this progression of sin when he wrote: " 'Come now, and let us reason together,' says the LORD, 'though your sins are like scarlet, they shall be as white as snow; though they are red like crimson, they shall be as wool' " (Isaiah 1:18). Isaiah was not only a prophet, he also served as tutor or spiritual advisor to four kings of Judah. He was fully aware of the law's teaching on identifying leprosy. The law stated that any Hebrew who had a red spot on his or her flesh must go to the priests for an examination. After an initial inspection, the priest isolated them for seven days following which they were reexamined by the priest.

> *And the priest shall look at him; and indeed if the*
> *swelling on the skin is white, and it has turned*
> *the hair white, and there is a spot of raw flesh in*
> *the swelling, it is an old leprosy on the skin of his*
> *body. The priest shall pronounce him unclean ...*
> (Leviticus 13:10-11).

The progression of leprosy was from red to white.

Isaiah used this as an analogy of the progression of sin. Initially sin may be little more than a redness in the skin, but given time to progress it will putrefy the flesh. Sin never gets better. Sin never turns from red to white; it turns the sinner from a lesser stage to a worse one. This verse is not an evangelistic text that speaks of cleansing from sin. The entire context of this chapter speaks of progressive departure from God and the subsequent consequences of that sin. God is not in the business of changing the color of sin, for white sin is as destructive as red sin. Rather than wash sin, God washes the repentant ones. He cleanses sin from our lives, casting it behind His back and removing every trace of its power.

Israel was unaware of this progression of sin into their lives. The prophet said, "Aliens have devoured his strength, but he does not know it; yes, gray hairs are here and there on him, yet he does not know it" (Hosea 7:9). The strength diminished so gradually that Israel learned to accommodate the resultant weakness without remembering the former strength. So preoccupied did they become with their idolatry that they overlooked the appearances of gray hair on their heads. This is almost incredulous, and yet sin can do this to any of us.

The prophet Hosea gave other similes for Israel's participation in idolatry without recognizing the changes it was producing in the nation. He called Israel a "silly dove" (7:11), a "deceitful bow" (7:16), a nation "swallowed up" by others (8:8), and a "wild donkey" (8:9). None of this is flattering, but sin lacks the power to create beauty. It can only degrade and destroy.

Israel replaced God's covenants

This downward progression of sin became evident in the nation of Israel. From adopting limited idolatry while learning to farm, the people blatantly built altars to the pagan gods of the land. It is, of course, one thing to build altars for sinning, and still another thing to worship at these altars. There will always be those who are merely observers of the sins of others, but most persons who are curious enough to watch soon find themselves stirred sufficiently to become willing participants. Israel not only looked at the idolaters, they lusted to become participants in the sensual rituals they watched. Desire soon became deed, and they became very accomplished in the art of idolatry — even creating their own idols. God spoke of this craft through Isaiah saying:

> *To whom then will you liken God? Or what likeness will you compare to Him? The workman molds a graven image, the goldsmith overspreads it with gold, and the silversmith casts silver chains. Whoever is too impoverished for such a contribution chooses a tree that will not rot; he seeks for himself a skillful workman to prepare a carved image that will not totter* (Isaiah 40:18-20).

This skill was in direct defiance of the first Ten Commandments that God had given to Israel from Mount Sinai. God had clearly said:

> *You shall have no other gods before Me. You shall not make for yourself a carved image, or any likeness of anything that is in heaven above, or that is in the earth beneath, or that is in the water under the earth* (Exodus 20:3-4).

This was a covenant with God that Israel entered very soon after their deliverance from Egyptian slavery. With the passage of time,

> *... they rejected His statutes and His covenant that He had made with their fathers, and His testimonies which He had testified against them; they followed idols, became idolaters, and went after the nations who were all around them, concerning whom the LORD had charged them that they should not do like them* (2 Kings 17:15).

In their embracing of idols, it was obvious that they had ceased to believe in the LORD; so we would expect that they did not believe His Word either. Whenever a person's faith in the Person of God is shaken, his or her faith in the promises of God will also totter, for the greatness of God's Word is the greatness of God. What God says will never be more meaningful than who God is. Israel's departure from God inevitably induced a departure from the covenants made with God as surely as a divorced person feels released from any marital commitment made with his or her past partner.

The generation that departed from this covenant was far removed from the people who had embraced that covenant. Perhaps they did not feel a responsibility to honor commitments made by their forefathers. How dangerous it is to renounce all God's past dealings with His covenant people and live totally in the present. Covenants God made to past generations are as valid today as they were then if we will meet the conditions. Since God's revelation is consistently progressive, it is concertedly dependent upon what He has already revealed. We need to heed the repeated warning: "Those who ignore history are doomed to repeat it."

Throughout my years of ministry, I have watched doctrinal errors quickly creep into each new move of God — causing pain and destruction. However, I have never seen a "new" error. It is always something that the Church examined hundreds of years ago and rejected as unbiblical. Because of a renewed inspiration of the Spirit upon the lives of certain believers, they feel a sense of superiority that causes them to reject past revelations of truth. Their excuse is, "They didn't have what we have." That may or may not be true. But even if it is so, it is because they brought the earlier revelation of God to the body of believers.

What the mathematician knows today would make the father of mathematics look on with amazement; but mathematicians could not be where they are in this science without the work of the former master of math. All science is cumulative, and so is spiritual truth. When you and I throw out the past, we greatly limit our present, for God is an eternal **now**. We need to participate in what He has revealed in His past dealings with covenant people, as well as what He is now revealing and is going to reveal as we mature. God will not reveal anything to this generation that violates something He revealed to a prior generation. God's purpose of revelation is to make Himself known to those who love Him. Therefore, it is always progressive; no one has yet come into the fullness of the knowledge of God. We are students, not graduates.

Israel replaced the worship of God

The sacred recorder says of Israel: "... they followed idols, became idolaters, and went after the nations who were all around them, concerning whom the LORD had charged them that they should not do like them" (2 Kings 17:15). The nation of Israel observed, accommodated, accepted and finally adopted idolatry as a substitute for relationship with Jehovah. This is the standard course of sinning.

Their progression is as modern as a space walk. Like Israel, we first observe sin — often with a "tisk tisk." It may be so horrible that we stay up until two in the morning to watch it on television. Second, we begin to accommodate what we see as right for others, saying that we do not have the right to force our moral code upon them. As we begin to accommodate it as a normal lifestyle for another, we begin to accept it as proper behavior. Finally, we adopt it for ourselves.

We would have much less idolatry to fight against today if we had shunned it yesterday. Somehow we never embrace and adopt until we have looked and investigated. That with which Israel flirted, they later flaunted in God's face. And so do we!

The sacred historian adds:

> *So they left all the commandments of the LORD their God, made for themselves a molded image and two calves, made a wooden image and worshiped all the host of heaven, and served Baal* (2 Kings 17:16).

Their imaginations demanded an image, and those images fed their fertile imaginations. When they departed from serving their Creator, they substituted their own creation. The people who were the work of God's hands wanted to worship the work of their hands.

King Jeroboam introduced the final step of idolatry to Israel:

> *... He tore Israel from the house of David, and they made Jeroboam the son of Nebat king. Then Jeroboam drove Israel from following the LORD, and made them commit a great sin. For the children of Israel walked in all the sins of Jeroboam which he did; they did not depart from them, until the LORD removed Israel out of His sight, as He had said by all His servants the prophets* (2 Kings 17:21-23).

Although God anointed Jeroboam to become king over the northern tribes, Jeroboam replaced the worship of Jehovah with idolatry for political reasons. Next he replaced Jehovah with the golden calves. While we must never underestimate the power of a strong leader, we need to recognize that the new king merely gave the people what their hearts desired — a substitute for God. There is no scriptural evidence that Jeroboam had to use any form of compulsion to get Israel to worship the calves once he set them in place. The people comfortably did what came naturally.

The calves became a substitute religion. An image of a domesticated animal over which man was given dominion replaced the God who has dominion over the lives of men and women. Jeroboam made his religion work and successfully prevented Israel from having any association with Jehovah's religion and the worship at the Temple in Jerusalem. His action is a dramatic type of the contrast between the true and the false church. We will always have both. The false church copies many of the rites and rituals of the true Church, but it maintains a separation of its people from the people of God.

The false church does much of what the true Church does. They sing, dance, do good deeds and have inspired utterances, prophecies and, occasionally, miracles. They are often very religious in their approach to life. To accommodate a wider range of adherents, it makes available a wide variety of formats from the very cold and formal to the very warm and active. Its style of worship encompasses both the rigid liturgical and the extreme free form. Like the chameleon that changes its color to blend into the background, the false church will quickly adapt to the current religious expression.

True saints will not embrace everything that seems to act correctly, for the false church is a master at acting. The issue is not the way they sing, dance, praise, or even worship. The issue that separates the true from the false church is the object of that worship. Any worship that does not go directly to God is false worship, no matter how beautiful, solemn or charismatic it may be.

The false church may evidence great growth that appears to be an evangelistic ministry, but it doesn't talk about sin, suffering or submission. It has no Christ and no cost. It speaks of pleasure, inherent goodness and the authority of man over his destiny. It offers salvation by the work of our own hands. It does not offer a cross, except as ornamentation. Instead, it offers a calf — a golden calf.

Israel replaced God

Jeroboam was aware of the power a golden calf had exerted on the people of Israel at Sinai, so he chose the same visible image; but he made two instead of one. Those calves made his religion work — they almost always do. That is why all religions have their golden calves. Unfortunately, although they are effective, they are a replacement for God.

The Hebrews first discovered calf worship in Egypt when they were slaves. Right after their exodus, they met Jehovah at Mount Sinai in the greatest demonstration of God that had ever been seen. There were wonders, signs, angels, heavenly trumpets, divine fire and the voice of Jehovah speaking directly to His covenant people. In awe, the congregation of Israel pledged to obey everything that God said.

In spite of all this, when Moses disappeared into the cloud of glory on the mountain to receive the law that God carved into stone with blazing fingers, the people demanded a visual representation of the God whose voice they had heard and whose Being they had sensed. They wanted something they could see and touch. Rather than withstand them, Aaron, whom Moses had left in charge, succumbed to the demands of the people and chose the calf over all the images he could have formed to represent God. Some writers suggest that Aaron deliberately chose this Egyptian deity hoping the people would be repelled by it. Instead, they found themselves attracted to it. It was something familiar. It was a visible representation — a result of their giving and the work of their hands. They could relate to the calf better than to the invisible God who had been giving and doing for them.

As a further deterrent to that action, Aaron insisted that the calf could be cast only from the golden earrings the people were then wearing. Slaves do not wear gold. Only the priesthood wore golden earrings in Egypt. It was a visible symbol of their power to hear from their gods. When the Egyptian priests could not stop Jehovah's plagues upon their land, they had to admit that they could not hear from their gods. As the Israelites left the land, the priests gladly gave their earrings to them as visible tokens that Israel heard from God, and that the Egyptian priests had lost their ability to hear divine messages. In effect, Aaron insisted that the people surrender their ability to hear from Jehovah so he could make an image to replace Him. They gladly surrendered their earrings and never heard the voice of God again. From that day on they were completely dependent upon Moses to hear God's voice as he shared it with them.

In every fresh move of God, there is an initial season when the people are hungry to hear from and about God. Those with teaching ministries find themselves in great demand. After awhile, however, people begin to lust for something more demonstrative. They tend to strip from their ears their authority to hear from God. They seem to be content to hand over that authority to some visual idol who claims to have great power, vision or abilities.

The charismatic renewal demonstrated this. The "electronic church" became the golden calf that replaced the great teaching conventions. It took millions of "earrings" to build and maintain those calves. Every time those golden calves seemed about to topple, more gold was requested to undergird them. It always came. They represented the kind of god we wanted to serve instead of introducing us to Jehovah God as He really is. These "ministries" were a visible representation of our sacrificial giving and the work of our hands. Perhaps the greatest tragedy of that issue is the amount of gold drained from widows, pensioners and welfare recipients to build and maintain them.

My wife and I have a long-term relationship with a precious person whom we have had to help financially from time to time. This dear saint, who has walked with God for years and has seen the glorious reality of God's presence in days past, considers it essential to send money every month to ministries that we know are golden calves. No sharing of our knowledge will change his mind. He merely thinks we are jealous. Repeatedly, in order to "get a word from God," he will write letters to the directors of these golden calves, totally unaware that the person he writes to will never even see the letter. A staff person prints out a form letter on a computer, which is then received as a word from God through the great prophet.

One of the powerful lies of false religions is that the giver has no responsibility over his gift. Like the children of Israel who gave their gold to Aaron to do whatever he chose to do with it, we pass our money on without ever checking to see what is done with it. "But I gave it to God," you might say. Unless the recipient was a true representative of God, the Lord never received the money. In the case of Israel's first calf at Sinai, the gold that went into constructing the calf had been provided for the construction of the Tabernacle in the Wilderness. Instead, Israel used God's provision of gold to construct a replacement for God. One wonders just how much more magnificent that Tabernacle might have been if Israel had given that gold to God instead of Aaron.

The life of Israel's first golden calf was very short. God sent Moses down from the mountain to stop the idolatrous worship. He not only punished the people, but he broke the calf to pieces, burned it, ground it into powder, threw it into the water supply and made the people drink it. Perhaps Moses reasoned that if the people wanted a false god, he would give them a belly full of that calf. Unfortunately, however, this action was not repeated with the calves of Jeroboam. Although God mercifully sent prophets to Israel, provided God-fearing kings among them, and even gave them great revival, nothing or no one ever dethroned the calves in Israel. They remained in place as a continuing plague until the day the Assyrians came to take them into slavery.

Similarly, no move of God in Church history has ever dethroned the false church. Somehow demons and men maintain their control over people with their golden substitutes for God. Revivals come and go, but religion and golden calves remain forever. It must be that the human heart has a propensity for holding on to something short of God — even if we have to make that "something" with our own hands.

Unquestionably one of the reasons for the perpetuity of religious calves is that their use is such an insidious replacement of God as to satisfy every religious desire without requiring a change of life. The Bible records:

> *Jeroboam ordained a feast on the fifteenth day of the eighth month, like the feast that was in Judah, and offered sacrifices on the altar. So he did at Bethel, sacrificing to the calves that he had made. And at Bethel he installed the priests of the high places which he had made. So he made offerings on the altar which he had made at Bethel on the fifteenth day of the eighth month, in the month which he had devised in his own heart. And he ordained a feast for the children of Israel, and offered sacrifices on the altar and burned incense* (1 Kings 12:32-33).

Jeroboam provided almost everything the people had come to expect at a festival unto God. There was a sacred day, a priesthood, sacrifices and the burning of incense. The fundamental difference was golden calves had replaced Jehovah.

Tragically, people will go through familiar forms, rituals and ceremonies and think they are having a spiritual experience whether God is present or not. Religious exercise will satisfy the soul, but only God Himself can meet the need of the human spirit. The Word of God declares: "The Spirit Himself bears witness with our spirit that we are children of God ..." (Romans 8:16) — a witness of Spirit with spirit, not Spirit with soul. Music, architecture, ritual and ceremony can definitely induce a response in the soul of persons; but only God can touch the spirit of men and women with transforming, elevating power.

God warned Israel that "... they shall be greatly ashamed, who trust in carved images, who say to the molded images, 'You are our gods' " (Isaiah 42:17). Later, when Israel was unable to cope with approaching enemies, they cried out to Jehovah for help. God said: "But where are your gods that you have made for yourselves? Let them arise, if they can save you in the time of your trouble ..." (Jeremiah 2:28)

Worship of anything short of God leaves us without the help of Almighty God in time of distress. Worshiping golden calves may meet emotional needs, but the rest of our lives remain vulnerable to attack without any available defense from the God we worship. Golden calves take, but they do not give anything back. When one calf fails us, we will turn to another, for like Israel, we will find it necessary to add more and more gods to our idolatrous worship.

When we exchange the worship of a Holy God for worship of the impure idols of the world, we can only expect our worship to become increasingly degenerate; for what began as a broad level road soon becomes a steep grade leading downward. Every step brings us to a lower act of worship that is more perverse than the preceding one.

Little children, keep yourselves from idols. Amen (1 John 5:21).

Chapter 7

The Perversity of Israel

Everything is black or white — good or evil — for some persons. The realist in life has discovered that there are shades or degrees between these extremes. Our criminal laws recognize different degrees of guilt, and God clearly points out distinct stages in righteousness. It was bad enough that the previous residents of the Promised Land were idol worshipers. To have those who had known the true and living God forsake Him in order to worship false substitutes was a far greater evil in the eyes of the Lord. Through the prophet Jeremiah, God cried,

> *For My people have committed two evils: they have forsaken Me, the fountain of living waters, and hewn themselves cisterns — broken cisterns that can hold no water. ... Those who depart from Me shall be written in the earth, because they have forsaken the LORD, the fountain of living waters* (Jeremiah 2:13; 17:13).

Israel had departed from the fresh, running streams of God for the stagnant, leaky cisterns of idolatry.

Viewing a departure from a living relationship with Christ, Peter declared:

> *For it would have been better for them not to have known the way of righteousness, than having known it, to turn from the holy commandment delivered to them* (2 Peter 2:21).

God speaks even more sternly in the letter to the Hebrew Christians:

> *For it is impossible for those who were once enlightened, and have tasted the heavenly gift, and have become partakers of the Holy Spirit, and have tasted the good word of God and the powers of the age to come, if they fall away, to renew them again to repentance, since they crucify again for themselves the Son of God, and put Him to an open shame* (Hebrews 6:4-6).

In God's sight, idolatry is never excusable; but Israel's idolatry was totally inexcusable. That nation of people knew better. They had tasted divine reality. They had benefited from generations of the blessing and providential care of Almighty God. Their departure was deliberate and diabolical; they did not merely succumb to a momentary temptation. Progressively calculating their moves, they knew what they were doing and should have known the results of those deeds, for they could see the repercussions for similar deeds in the nations around them. They were not pioneering new territory; they were regressing into the patterns God had consistently condemned.

So much of what we learn in life is by observation. Long before children understand words, they learn by watching others. Even after we mature, we remember more of what we see than what we hear. Isn't it sad, then, that persons refuse to learn about the tragic consequences of sin by observing the captives of sin? No rational person in our society can say he or she did not realize where sinful actions would lead them. Television dramatizes it as entertainment. Our hospitals and mental care units overflow with individuals who are reaping the wages of sin. We are not ignorant; we are deliberate. The momentary pleasures of sin with its artificial glamor detract our attention from the gruesome results that sin will produce. The full ramifications of sin are evident, but we are willfully blind to them. Participation in sin is not an act of ignorance; it is a willful performance.

Israel did not enter idolatry ignorantly. The steps from God to Baal, although progressive, were deliberate. Israel chose to go the way of other nations. It was predictable, then, that those acts of idolatry would lead to the same extreme perversion to be seen in those heathen nations. Knowing that His people were willfully blind, God sent prophet after prophet with pleadings and warnings, but those who chose not to see were also determined not to listen. God had no option except to let them sink lower and lower into the depravity of idolatry. History records the depth of perversity that Israel eventually reached before God sent the nation into captivity.

Israel worshiped creation instead of the Creator

The sacred scribe tells us they "... worshiped all the host of heaven..." (2 Kings 17:16) Past and present generations have been overwhelmed by the canopy of stars God spread over us. Recently, I enjoyed a rafting trip down the Colorado River with two of my brothers. At night we slept in our sleeping bags on a sandbar deep in the Grand Canyon. We witnessed the blackness of the canyon and the contrastingly bright shining of the stars. The sight was overpowering. The three of us almost involuntarily began to praise the Lord audibly. We probably experienced the emotions David felt when he wrote:

When I consider Your heavens, the work of Your fingers, the moon and the stars, which You have ordained, What is man that You are mindful of him, and the son of man that You visit him? (Psalm 8:3-4)

All nature declares the glory of God. Paul said that even without a revelation of Jesus Christ, all people of the world are without excuse because God has revealed Himself through His creation. Romans 1:18-20 declares:

For the wrath of God is revealed from heaven against all ungodliness and unrighteousness of men, who suppress the truth in unrighteousness, because what may be known of God is manifest in them, for God has shown it to them. For since the creation of the world His invisible attributes are clearly seen, being understood by the things that are made, even His eternal power and God-head, so that they are without excuse.

It is not the gospel that reveals God; it is creation. Paul declares in Romans 1:16-17 that the gospel reveals the righteousness of God:

For I am not ashamed of the gospel of Christ, for it is the power of God to salvation for everyone who believes, for the Jew first and also for the Greek. For in it the righteousness of God is revealed from faith to faith; as it is written, "The just shall live by faith."

No missionary need travel to unknown lands to convince persons of the reality of God. How can one view creation without an awareness there must be a creator? It is the person of God and His demonstrated love in becoming our righteousness that forms the message of the missionary. Mankind needs to know what Paul wrote to the Corinthian church:

But of Him you are in Christ Jesus, who became for us wisdom from God — and righteousness and sanctification and redemption. ... For He made Him who knew no sin to be sin for us, that we might become the righteousness of God in Him (1 Corinthians 1:30; 2 Corinthians 5:21).

Although the glory of creation should bring us to the Creator, idolatry substitutes the worship of the cosmos for the worship of Christ. Israel, to whom God had revealed Himself in multiple ways, chose to worship the sun, moon, stars and constellations rather than the One who created them all. They fell into the trap of astrology when they walked away from the truth of Almighty God.

Astrology is certainly not new. The Old Testament shows us that heathen kings kept astrologers on their staffs of advisors. Right after bringing Israel out of Egypt, God told them, "For these nations which you will dispossess listened to soothsayers and diviners; but as for you, the LORD your God has not appointed such for you" (Deuteronomy 18:14). More than once, God condemned the use of nature in an attempt to look into the future, but Israel refused to listen seriously. After they had turned from worshiping the Creator to the worship of creation, God told them:

You are wearied in the multitude of your counsels; let now the astrologers, the stargazers, and the monthly prognosticators stand up and save you from these things that shall come upon you (Isaiah 47:13).

When covenant people seek knowledge from the handiwork of God rather than from God Himself, the Lord often delivers them to their own devises so they may discover that these devices are lying deceptions.

Christians need to know that there is nothing "innocent" in using the astrological charts. Their use is an attempt to find guidance apart from God. It puts their lives into the hands of "fate" instead of into the hands of a loving, merciful heavenly Father. Americans experiment with astrology. Our daily newspapers carry astrological charts, and those publishers who dare to discontinue them meet with such an outrage of public opinion that they have to reinstate them.

It was shocking to Christians to learn that while Ronald Reagan was President of the United States, he regularly consulted an astrologer through his wife, Nancy, before making important decisions of state. Hypocritically, many of those same Christians regularly check the chart in the daily paper "just for fun."

Astrology is not a science; it is a religion — a false religion. The Bible declares it to be a form of idolatry. It is the first form of idolatry described after Israel formed the golden calves as a replacement for Jehovah. Christians must learn to appreciate God's creation without being deceived into worshiping it instead of God Himself. Otherwise we will find ourselves in idolatry, just as Israel did.

Israel traded love for lust

"... they ... served Baal" (2 Kings 17:16) is the cry of a brokenhearted God. God consistently declared to Israel: "I have loved you..." (Malachi 1:2) He chose them to be His special people when He called Abraham out of Chaldea, and He exerted very special care over them throughout the forthcoming generations. When they were but a family, God demonstrated His paternal love for them. As they later grew and multiplied in Egypt, Jehovah led them forth with a mighty hand of deliverance and made them into a nation. God's providential care for them in the wilderness, in spite of their repeated murmurings, insurrections and pleas to be allowed to return to Egypt, underscored the unconditional nature of the divine love. He told them: "Yes, I have loved you with an everlasting love; therefore with lovingkindness I have drawn you" (Jeremiah 31:3).

Just as the New Testament proclaims the love of Jesus for His Church, the Old Testament heralds the love of Jehovah for Israel. It is, of course, the same message, but God chose the Hebrews to be an open demonstration of this sacred *agape*. Through Israel, Jehovah displayed to the entire world what Paul said the Church needs to learn: "... what is the width and length and depth and height − to know the love of Christ which passes knowledge; that you may be filled with all the fullness of God" (Ephesians 3:18-19).

God has never been satisfied merely to be known as the God of love. He yearns for mankind to know the love of God. Since love can never be academically absorbed, God deliberately displayed His love to Israel by attitude, action and affirmation. God told them through the prophet:

> *For I am the LORD your God, the Holy One of Israel, your Savior; I gave Egypt for your ransom, Ethiopia and Seba in your place. Since you were precious in My sight, you have been honored, and I have loved you; therefore I will give men for you, and people for your life* (Isaiah 43:3-4).

It is difficult to understand why Israel would ever disown such love to serve Baal. Even Jehovah asks: "Can a virgin forget her ornaments, or a bride her attire? Yet My people have forgotten Me days without number" (Jeremiah 2:32). Yet Israel did just that. That nation deliberately turned from serving Jehovah, from whom all blessings flowed, to serving the heathen god

Baal, to whom they gave credit for those benefits. Admittedly, the transition was gradual, but it was progressive.

Baal, which means "possessor, owner, master, lord or husband," was a title given to many local deities worshiped by the inhabitants of Canaan. In Joshua's time, the Canaanites considered Baal synonymous with Hadad the bull, a symbol of fertility, and, as "the son of Dagan," the fertility god worshiped by the Philistines. They viewed him as having absolute control of fertility in agriculture, animals and mankind. As stated earlier, the practice of agriculture involved the offering of sacrifices to this god, and, of course, the harvest was credited to his favor. Since the Hebrews learned to farm from their neighbors, that led to the adoption of Baal worship as an act of business. Initially all Baal worship was done in innocence. Israel viewed Jehovah as the God of provision in the wilderness, but Baal became the symbol of provision in the land. While using the name of Baal, the early settlers were still thinking of Jehovah. As time progressed, Israel's worship of Jehovah became Canaanized to the extent that they appended the attributes and even the name of Baal to Jehovah. *The Zondervan Pictorial Encyclopedia of the Bible* says: "The northern kingdom was more susceptible to the inroads of the native Canaanite cults than was the more isolated and largely agricultural kingdom of Judah." It adds: "This tendency was probably accelerated by the sensuous appeal of the Canaanite cults" (Volume 1, page 433).

Whatever innocence may have initiated Israel's response to Baal disappeared as they continued to worship that fertility god. During the reign of Ahab, his wife Jezebel, a Phoenician princess, determined to obliterate Jehovah worship and make Baal the official god. Ahab built temples to Baal at Samaria and in Jerusalem. Those temples contained an image of the fertility god in the shape of a pillar and Baal worshipers wore special vestments. Incense altars to Baal were erected in the streets of Jerusalem, and the people burned incense to Baal on the flat roofs of their houses (see Jeremiah 32:29). Ahab and Jezebel almost succeeded in their attempt to replace Jehovah with Baal, for God admitted to Elijah that He had but 7000 Israelites who remained true to Him (see 1 Kings 19:18). Israel would have completely departed from the worship of Jehovah if it were not for the intervention of God through Elijah. Elijah's destruction of the priests and prophets of Baal, after calling fire from heaven upon the sacrifice to Jehovah, slowed Israel's embracing of Baalism, but it did not destroy it.

The Scriptures leave no doubt that the strong attraction of Baal worship was its ritual prostitution. Although Balaam failed in his attempt to curse Israel at the request of Balak, he advised Balak to get Israel involved in the worship of Baal. That slowly accomplished what he had hoped to do by cursing the multitude of God's chosen people, for it introduced Israel to sexual sensuality as an act of worship. We read:

Then Israel remained in Acacia Grove, and the people began to commit harlotry with the women of Moab. They invited the people to the sacrifices of their gods, and the people ate and bowed down to their gods. So Israel was joined to Baal of Peor, and the anger of the LORD was aroused against Israel (Numbers 25:1-3).

Although God condemned all the men who participated in that cultic adultery to immediate death, the attractiveness of religious sexuality was not destroyed. As early as the generation following Joshua, God said: "... they played the harlot with other gods, and bowed down to them" (Judges 2:17). No amount of prophetic warnings or divine chastisement could eradicate that lusting from the Israelites. God said of Israel:

"My people ask counsel from their wooden idols, and their staff informs them. For the spirit of harlotry has caused them to stray, and they have played the harlot against their God" (Hosea 4:12). A little later in this book God again says, "For the spirit of harlotry is in their midst, and they do not know the LORD" (Hosea 5:4).

While the Bible mocks the uselessness of carved or molten idols, declaring them to be without life, it also indicates that behind these images often lurk evil spirits that accept the worship and energize the worshipers. Through the prophet Hosea, God said that early experimentation with Baal worship opened the people to the spirit behind that idol. As a result, they became hopelessly infected with "the spirit of harlotry." Israel was so inflamed with the spirit of harlotry that God said, "They are all adulterers. Like an oven heated by a baker ... They prepare their heart like an oven ... They are all hot, like an oven ..." (Hosea 7:4,6,7)

So perverted had their form of worship become that God observed: "... A man and his father go in to the same girl, to defile My holy name" (Amos 2:7). Unfortunately it was not only the men who were religiously immoral. God said:

> *Therefore your daughters commit harlotry, and your brides commit adultery. I will not punish your daughters when they commit harlotry, nor your brides when they commit adultery; for the men themselves go apart with harlots, and offer sacrifices with a ritual harlot* (Hosea 4:13-14).

In light of recent revelations of gross sexual impurity among key religious leaders in the major countries of the world, this is extremely applicable to the worship of today's Church. The spirit of harlotry still inflames the passions of men and women who once walked in pure covenant relationship with God. Far wiser men than myself have observed that satan sends these three to every man of God: a witch who seeks to dominate him, a prostitute who seeks to defile him, and a parasite who seeks to drain him. The prostitute is often the most successful of the three.

Satan has always sought to put lust into religion. While I was writing this chapter, I was ministering in a very victorious worship convention in the heart of Brussels, Belgium. We had secured the facilities of a downtown Anglican cathedral located in the wealthy district of that capital city. I was shocked to see two topless clubs immediately next to the old church. Nude pictures, flashing lights and doormen inviting patrons to come inside were seen by the church members as they left the evening services. Judging from the cars parked on the streets, the clientele was affluent. Once again satan had put prostitution right next to religion. On the final evening of the conference, we experienced a noisy demonic demonstration during the worship that followed the teaching. When the demons were commanded to come out of two women, they declared that they were commissioned to come and disrupt the service. One of the women admitted, after she was delivered, that she was a prostitute.

The adultery and sexual impurity in the modern Church grieves God as much as did Israel's degraded worship. God said of His beloved people:

> ... I was crushed by their adulterous heart which has departed from Me, and by their eyes which play the harlot after their idols; they will loathe themselves for the evils which they committed in all their abominations (Ezekiel 6:9).

Israel violated the sanctity of life

Cruelty reigns where satan is king. When idolatry is the dominant religion of a country, there is a progressive degeneration of its citizens. Women are degraded, the poor are exploited, the sick are not cared for, and the aged and infirm are abandoned to die. To add to this horror, children are often sacrificed to the gods of the land. While Christ died to regenerate humanity, satan delights in degenerating them. Although the gospel elevates people to new heights, sin lowers persons to greater depths. The apparent pleasures of sin carry a tremendous price tag.

It is inconceivable that a nation of people who had been delivered from the degradation of slavery by Almighty God could ever lower themselves to offer human sacrifices to a lifeless idol. That they offered their children instead of themselves is totally despicable. The sacrifice of the innocent for the sake of the guilty is the backbone of substitutionary atonement. God provided animal sacrifices for that purpose until the time of Christ — He became the ultimate sacrificial substitution for sinning persons.

Although Israel had the law and full understanding of the sacrificial provision of Jehovah, when they gave themselves to worship Baal "... they caused their sons and daughters to pass through the fire ..." (2 Kings 17:17) That was an intrinsic part of worship for the Phoenicians, and common as well to the Moabites, Ammonites and other nations that surrounded Israel. Some writers have declared that it was merely a dedication ceremony in which children passed between two fires as an act of consecration to the perpetual service of a heathen god as priests and priestesses or as temple prostitutes. Neither the Bible nor history confirms this projection. God declared: "... they have also built the high places of Baal, to burn their sons with fire for burnt offerings to Baal, which I did not command or speak, nor did it come into My mind" (Jeremiah 19:5).

The records of historians make it clear that this was no innocent ceremony, but did, indeed, involve the incineration of the living children. One writer describes the ceremony as it took place at the Phoenician colony of Carthage. In the temple of Saturn (Moloch in the Old Testament) was a metal image in the form of a human figure with a bull's head and extended arms. When the idol became glowing hot from the fire in its interior, priests laid the sacrificial children in its arms to be roasted to death or rolled from the arms into the fire inside the idol. No grief could be displayed by the parents, for they lost the honor of the act if they wept or sobbed. The sacrifice continued without any interruptions. The noise of musical instruments drowned out the children's pitiful cries of agony. Is it possible that a similar sacrifice of children is occurring in America today among Christians and non-Christians alike? Even beyond the thousands of unborn children that are sacrificed daily by abortion, we sacrifice the living children to various forms of idolatry. We sacrifice their minds by giving our children to godless educators to shape their thinking in idolatrous patterns. We release them to sit mindlessly in front of the television screen — unsupervised for hours each day — and allow them to view things God's Word clearly prohibits (all in the name of entertainment). Even when we bring our children to church with us, they "play" in children's church while the parents worship God in the auditorium. We often sacrifice our children in our idolatrous worship of the god of lust. Christian counselors report that the rampant growth of incest in America is high among Christian families and rapidly increasing. Perhaps God would say of modern Christians what He regretfully said to the errant Hebrews: "... you have slain My children and offered them up to them [idols] by causing them to pass through the fire" (Ezekiel 16:21).

Do we think that the devil will ignore our intensive worship of God if he can claim our children? He won't! If we continue to sacrifice the second generation to the gods of the land, we will never fulfill the great commission the Lord gave to the Church. We dare not start over every third generation. We need the seed of God to grow, develop, mature and continue to bring forth fruit generation after generation. When Pharaoh finally allowed Moses and the men to go into the wilderness to worship God, Moses said, "We will go with our young and our old; with our sons and our daughters, with our flocks and our herds we will go, for we must hold a feast to the LORD" (Exodus 10:9). May God grant us the same boldness in dealing with the gods of this world. We will not sacrifice our children. We will serve God as family units.

Israel replaced worship with witchcraft

Magical practices always accompanied idolatry, so it is not too surprising to read: "... they ... practiced witchcraft and soothsaying ..." (2 Kings 17:17) Where faith in God abates, a trust in magical practices abounds. Persons who refuse to hear the voice of the Lord will seek another voice just as King Saul sought instruction from the dead through the witch of Endor when he discovered that God's voice was no longer available to him.

It is dangerous to open ourselves to be filled with the Spirit of God unless we intend to go all the way with God. Once our spirit learns to contact the spirit realm, it will demand such a contact. We create a vacuum in our spirits that yearns to be filled when we abandon God. If the Holy Spirit does not fill it, a demon spirit may very well fill it. Having once enjoyed and participated in guidance and provision beyond ourselves, there is no satisfaction without it. When Israel turned from Jehovah, who had liberated, led, fed and taught them, it created a void that needed to be filled. They turned to witchcraft to meet that need.

Many people sit in Pentecostal and Charismatic churches today who once spoke ecstatically under the inspiration of the Holy Spirit; but now they speak in tongues by action of demonic spirits. Unfortunately some persons are foolish enough to seek interpretation of those utterances. It demonstrates that when we live in rebellion against God, we usually don't know the difference between the divine voice and the voice of demons.

Israel turned to witchcraft for guidance in life after they departed from God, much as Saul had in their earlier history. Most of our major churches today have at least one witch in them now, and more are coming. Sweet, lovely, gracious, Bible-talking witches are invading our churches and deceiving us with their gentleness and Bible quotations. If the Church of Jesus Christ ever needed the discerning of spirits, we need it now. Merely judging a communication by comparing it to the Bible is not sufficient, for the New Age people, witches and warlocks quote the Bible consistently. Paul told the Corinthians: "And no wonder! For satan himself transforms himself into an angel of light" (2 Corinthians 11:14). We need the combined witness of the Living Word with the written Word if we are to escape the delusion the enemy is now introducing into our churches.

There is presently a lusting for a "word from God" in many of our Charismatic churches. Likely this is connected to a departure from purity and a rampant disobedience to the Word of God. Disillusioned people are turning to the religious idols we have set up in our midst to seek guidance for their lives. We have so glamorized the reception of "a word of knowledge" or a personal prophecy that little judging of either takes place. I fear that what some leaders declare to be the work of the Holy Spirit is a modern form of witchcraft.

Currently there is a major emphasis upon the prophetic gift, and many groups are raising up prophets — even conducting schools to train persons to be prophets. There are more prophets in America today than in any previous generation. Whenever there is a yearning in the Church, the enemy rises with a substitute answer to satisfy that yearning.

This is not an indictment against true prophecy. The Bible declares: "Do not despise prophecies" (1 Thessalonians 5:20). We should not blindly accept everything that purports to be a "word" from God, no matter how pleasing it may sound. Paul taught: "Test all things; hold fast what is good" (1 Thessalonians 5:21). Witchcraft is not always connected with incantations around an open fire. In enlightened circles, it often wears a far more religious garb in communicating with closet idolaters.

Israel exchanged righteousness for evil

God describes the final progression of this downward step into idolatry in the simple statement: "they ... sold themselves to do evil in the sight of the Lord ..." (2 Kings 17:17) The imagery of this statement comes from the institutions of slavery where the bondservant was wholly at his master's disposal and was bound to fulfill his will. Paul referred to this as well when he wrote: "For we know that the law is spiritual, but I am carnal, sold under sin" (Romans 7:14).

When Israel departed from the service of Jehovah, they became bondslaves to the evil of idolatry. There was no righteousness left, nor was there any desire to do righteously. Depravity is the result of departure from God. When the Law of God is rejected, all standards of holiness disappear — as we have repeatedly witnessed in the history of the Church on earth.

Iniquity is not always self-evident. It masks itself as pleasure and clothes itself with respectability. The effects of its evil often move slowly in the nature of the participant while remaining hidden from view. However, evil, like drugs, must have an increased intensity to continue to give pleasure. Unlike the married couple who make a covenant to settle down to a lifetime together, evil continues to seek new companions, fresh partners and deeper involvements. Rebellion is always seeking greater expression. In the practice of idolatry, you cannot draw the line — declaring this is as far as you will go — because when you do, it no longer gives pleasure.

I was traveling in the Orient some years ago with a dear brother from Canada who has now gone on to be with the Lord. Finding ourselves with a free day after weeks of intensive ministry, he suggested that we go to a quality restaurant and have something to eat. The waitress automatically brought a bottle of saki to our table when we placed our order. Our limited knowledge of Japanese prevented us from successfully communicating to her that we did not want this, so we merely set the bottle aside. My friend explained to me that he was confident it would not greatly disturb God if he took a drink of saki. He had two brothers and a father who died alcoholics, and he had chosen not to give alcohol a chance to ruin his life, too. If only the Church would be that wise. Surely we have seen how a little flirtation with immorality has destroyed others. Why flirt with it? Even modern history of the Church will reveal what departure from the Scriptures has done to individuals. Do we think ourselves stronger than they? All entrance into idolatry encompasses the potential of selling ourselves to do evil.

Among the final statements in the Bible is the sad approbation: "He who is unjust, let him be unjust still; he who is filthy, let him be filthy still; he who is righteous, let him be righteous still; he who is holy, let him be holy still" (Revelation 22:11). There comes a time when God releases us to our own lustful desires. As he said of Israel, "Ephraim is joined to idols, let him alone" (Hosea 4:17). That was not approval. It was abandonment. Far from approving Israel's embracing of idolatry, God extracted a severe penalty for her altars for sinning.

Little children, keep yourselves from idols. Amen (1 John 5:21).

Chapter 8

The Penalty Israel Paid for Worshiping Idols

From the safety of a cleft in a rock, Moses asked to see God "and the LORD passed before him and proclaimed, 'The LORD, the LORD God, merciful and gracious, longsuffering, and abounding in goodness and truth ... ' " (Exodus 34:6) The very first attribute God used to describe Himself was *mercy*. Our very hope of survival is this inherent mercy of God. Even after observing the severe judgments of God upon Jerusalem, Jeremiah cried: "Through the Lord's mercies we are not consumed, because His compassions fail not" (Lamentations 3:22).

The psalmists declare the mercy of God nearly a hundred times. Psalm 136 ends every verse with the affirmation, "for His mercy endures forever," and the verse that sits in the exact center of our Bible declares,

"Mercy and truth have met together; righteousness and peace have kissed each other" (Psalm 85:10). David drank deeply at the well of God's abundant mercy. In trying to make others aware of the magnitude of that mercy, he wrote: "For as the heavens are high above the earth, so great is His mercy toward those who fear Him" (Psalm 103:11). The mercy of the Lord is immeasurable, inexplicable and inexhaustible, for God assures us His mercies "... are new every morning" (Lamentations 3:23).

Because of this vast reservoir of the grace of God, many have overlooked God's capacity for anger. The very man to whom God had proclaimed Himself to be inherently merciful experienced the anger of God more than once. Moses got acquainted with God's anger in the episode of the golden calf. That meekest of men first dealt with the sin in the camp that had stirred God's anger and then returned to God's presence on the mount to prostrate himself before God in earnest intercession that lasted forty days and nights. On later occasions, Moses again interceded with an angry God, for God's anger with sin flows from His holiness. God is inherently more holy than He is merciful. We never read of the angels proclaiming the mercy of God, but we frequently read how they declare the holiness of God. Sin, which violates God's holiness, causes Him to turn from a demonstration of mercy to a display of righteous anger. The herdsman prophet declared: "The Lord GOD has sworn by His holiness: 'Behold, the days shall come upon you when He will take you away with fishhooks, and your posterity with fishhooks' " (Amos 4:2). God based this oath on His holiness.

Israel's great sin was the violation of a covenant made with God. God views a covenant as a holy thing, even when it is between persons on this earth, but covenants between persons and God are especially holy. Desecration of the covenant sealed with God at

Mt. Sinai was an unforgivable encroachment upon God's holiness. The Bible teaches that it is far better to refuse to enter a covenant with God than to embrace such a covenant and default on it. Solomon wrote: "When you make a vow to God, do not delay to pay it; for He has no pleasure in fools. Pay what you have vowed" (Ecclesiastes 5:4).

God is just in His anger against any form of sin, for He has made complete provision for the eradication of sin in His covenant people. Repeatedly He has demonstrated that mercy to the people of His love. Still, when people consistently use God's grace as an excuse for disgrace, and interpret His mercy as consent, He releases His anger as a punitive measure. Even then His mercy is evident, for we would be destroyed if He did not control His anger.

No matter how controlled or tempered it may be, God's anger is difficult to endure. The prophet said: "But the LORD is the true God; He is the living God and the everlasting King. At His wrath the earth will tremble, and the nations will not be able to abide His indignation" (Jeremiah 10:10). David said: "Then the earth shook and trembled; the foundations of the hills also quaked and were shaken, because He was angry" (Psalm 18:7). Only a fool would fail to realize that it is dangerous to fall into the hands of an angry God.

The simple statement: "Therefore the LORD was very angry with Israel, and removed them from His sight; there was none left but the tribe of Judah alone" (2 Kings 17:18) expresses some of the harshest words to be found in the Bible. Instead of marveling at their final rejection, one wonders how a holy God could have borne with them for so long. For two centuries God showed mercy to that stiff-necked, stubborn people who seemed always set to ignore the ways of the Lord. God finally gave up on them and "was **very** angry with Israel."

God's anger is never to be taken lightly. Asaph, the psalmist, sang: "You, Yourself, are to be feared; and who may stand in Your presence when once You are angry?" (Psalm 76:7) Like the spoiled child who continues to push the limits of a parent's tolerance, Israel finally went over the line of God's extended grace and faced an angry God. They did not share David's plea: "O LORD, do not rebuke me in Your anger, nor chasten me in Your hot displeasure" (Psalm 6:1), so they found themselves sharing the lot of their forefathers of whom it is written:

He cast on them the fierceness of His anger, wrath, indignation, and trouble, by sending angels of destruction among them. He made a path for His anger; He did not spare their soul from death, but gave their life over to the plague (Psalm 78:49-50).

What we will not learn by observation, we must learn by experience. In dealing with God's anger, this is disastrous. God declares: "Now see that I, even I, am He, and there is no God besides Me; I kill and I make alive; I wound and I heal; nor is there any who can deliver from My hand" (Deuteronomy 32:39). Israel seriously underestimated the prerogative of an angry God.

Israel disappeared from God's sight

The sacred chronicler records: "Therefore the LORD ... removed them from His sight," and, "... the LORD removed Israel out of His sight" (2 Kings 17:18,23). It is serious enough to be unable to see God, but it is tragic when God chooses not to see us! The ironic justice in this is that those rebellious idolaters had said: "The LORD does not see, nor does the God of Jacob understand" (Psalm 94:7), and, "God has forgotten; He hides His face; He will never see it" (Psalm 10:11). They dared to persist in their worship at the altars for sinning, because they had convinced themselves that

Jehovah neither saw nor cared. In a sense, they chose their punishment. It is as if God merely did what they had declared Him to be doing — He turned His face from them.

It is ironic that God often responds to us as we have responded to Him. By building and worshiping at their altars for sinning, Israel forsook God; then God forsook Israel. The Israelites were seeking the face of another rather than the face of God, so God hid His face from them. They chose to worship a god of their making, so the God Who made them, eliminated Himself as their object of worship. He would neither see nor hear anything they did.

Removal from God's sight is loss of His favor and care. That is the one punishment David did not want. He was willing to fall into the chastising hands of God and suffer the consequences, but he cried: "Do not hide Your face from me; do not turn Your servant away in anger ..." (Psalm 27:9), and, "... Do not hide Your face from me, lest I be like those who go down into the pit" (Psalm 143:7). David could accept a spanking from God, but he did not want separation from Him.

When Jesus hung on the cross as our vicarious sacrifice, bearing all the sins of the world upon Himself, He bravely endured the mockery and the inhuman treatment He received. He gave no expression to the pain and shame of the cross. It was not until the Father turned His face from the Son that "... Jesus cried out with a loud voice, saying, 'Eli, Eli, lama sabachthani?' that is, 'My God, My God, why have You forsaken Me?' " (Matthew 27:46) For Christ Jesus, the worst part of the crucifixion was separation from the Father.

Whether we are mature enough to understand it or not, the worst thing God can do to any of us is to turn His face from us. Job realized this, for he cried, "Why do You hide Your face, and regard me as Your enemy?"

(Job 13:24) The psalmist also observed: "You hide Your face, they are troubled; You take away their breath, they die and return to their dust" (Psalm 104:29). When God turns His face from us, our very source of life disappears. Death is all that remains.

Isaiah said, "Truly You are God, who hide Yourself, O God of Israel, the Savior! They shall be ashamed and also disgraced, all of them; They shall go in confusion together, who are makers of idols" (Isaiah 45:15-16). It is the sin of idolatry that causes God to remove persons from His sight. The person who chooses to worship at the altars for sinning instead of the altar of God has already rejected the Lord as God and has set his or her affections on something far beneath the LORD.

Israel experienced permanent rejection

The second step in Israel's penalty for worshiping at altars for sinning was God's rejection: "And the LORD rejected all the descendants of Israel ..." (2 Kings 17:20) That author recorded those events long after they had transpired. With the benefit of hindsight, the writer could project the severity of the penalty God imposed upon Israel. It was not merely the generation that built and worshiped idols that experienced rejection. "God rejected all the descendants of Israel." God had warned the Hebrews of that penalty. When God verbally gave the Ten Commandments at Sinai, He said:

You shall not make for yourself any carved image, or any likeness of anything that is in heaven above, or that is in the earth beneath, or that is in the water under the earth; you shall not bow down to them nor serve them. For I, the LORD your God, am a jealous God, visiting the iniquity of the fathers on the children to the third and fourth generations of those who hate Me (Exodus 20:4-5).

Cruel as this may sound, God said that His judgment upon idolatry would affect at least four generations.

For those of us living in the grace of God, this seems inconsistent with the nature of God. Yet when God revealed His nature to Moses, He declared Himself as "... keeping mercy for thousands, forgiving iniquity and transgression and sin, by no means clearing the guilty, visiting the iniquity of the fathers upon the children and the children's children to the third and the fourth generation" (Exodus 34:7). Many years after this revelation, Jeremiah said to God, "You show lovingkindness to thousands, and repay the iniquity of the fathers into the bosom of their children after them" (Jeremiah 32:18).

Some interpret these verses to mean that the sins of the fathers so deeply affect their children that succeeding generations continue in that sin. This does let God off the hook, but it is not what the Bible says. God's punishment for the sin of idolatry goes into succeeding generations unless repentance releases that sin and righteousness replaces it. I have ministered in countries that are experiencing this long-term forsaking of God. The idolatrous acts of their fathers have left today's generation without a contract with God. How seldom do parents consider the consequences of forsaking God for current idols. While we have the right to accept or reject a relationship with God, we seldom realize that choosing altars to sin instead of altars of righteousness invokes the judgment of God upon our children. We not only introduce them into our rebellion against God, we incorporate them into God's judgment of our sin.

When Judah embraced idolatry, God sold them into Babylonian captivity for seventy years, but He brought them back and restored them as a nation.

God's dealings with Israel were different. When He rejected them as His covenant people, it was permanent. They went into Assyrian captivity never again to return to their land as a nation. The ten tribes sinned themselves into slavery, destitution and everlasting obscurity. Having said in their hearts to God, "Depart from us!" God said to them, "Depart from Me!" The divorce was complete.

There are, obviously, some decisions we make that affect us eternally. Just as God told King Saul, "Because you have rejected the word of the LORD, He also has rejected you from being king" (1 Samuel 15:23), so our rejection of God as the sole object of our worship sets the stage for God to reject us, even after He has crowned us "... kings and priests to His God and Father ..." (Revelation 1:6)

The mercy of God allows us to repent of wrong decisions and turn around our lives. Idolatry can be forsaken. Sin can be confessed and cleansed. Israel did not do this, for the nation not only embraced idols and built altars for sinning upon which to worship them, but that nation also forsook God. Jesus spoke of this when He said,

> *Many will say to Me in that day, "Lord, Lord, have we not prophesied in Your name, cast out demons in your name, and done many wonders in Your name?" And then I will declare to them, "I never knew you; depart from Me, you who practice lawlessness!"* (Matthew 7:22-23)

The great fallacy of religious idolatry is that no amount of good works can compensate for the lawlessness of worshiping anything other than Jehovah God. Once God removes us out of His sight, it is as though we had never met Him. We become foreigners and strangers to Him. We choose another, and He leaves us to our choices. There are no "friendly divorces" from

God. Unless there is a decided change on our part, the action is eternal.

Israel's enemies ravished the nation mercilessly

The author of Second Kings adds: "And the LORD ... afflicted them, and delivered them into the hand of the plunders ... " (2 Kings 17:20) While we usually see the Assyrians as God's tool in punishing Israel, the Bible says that before the enemy ever arrived on the scene, "the LORD afflicted them." It is bad enough to be afflicted physically like Paul, and it is worse to be plagued by the enemy like Job, but it is devastating when God afflicts us.

The Egyptians learned that God's plagues become progressively severe once Jehovah begins to afflict persons. Initially, God's afflictions are simply an inconvenience (the rivers turned to blood), but as they become increasingly severe, we become inconsolable (death of the firstborn). At first we cannot drink of the waters we have chosen, but God's hand of judgment relentlessly brings death to the rebellious ones. He who insists upon playing games with God is doomed to continual defeat. God has more ways to afflict idolaters than they have false gods to worship.

Calamity is never causeless. The book of wisdom says, "Like a flitting sparrow, like a flying swallow, so a curse without cause shall not alight" (Proverbs 26:2). Knowing that a curse is not always the result of personal action, we would still be wise to search our own hearts and lives for a possible cause if we are experiencing affliction. Far too often we blame demonic activity for things that have come from the hand of God. The mature Christian learns to deal with God first then waits for instructions from God before dealing with satan.

Affliction from the hand of the Lord comes upon churches as well. Christ said in His letter to the church at Ephesus: "Remember therefore from where you have fallen; repent and do the first works, or else I will come to you quickly and remove your lampstand from its place — unless you repent" (Revelation 2:5). Just as God removed Israel from their land, so Christ threatens to remove us from our place in His presence unless we repent. All forms of religious idolatry expose us to the severe affliction of the Lord. The congregation of persons who progressively abandons God as the sole object of their worship will discover that God progressively abandons them and deliberately afflicts them.

Must religion consistently go from deliverance out of Egypt into Assyrian captivity? When God used Israel to drive out the inhabitants of the Promised Land, He said they were "... seven nations greater and mightier than you, and when the LORD your God delivers them over to you, you shall conquer them and utterly destroy them ..." (Deuteronomy 7:1-2) As we now know, Israel conquered only such territory as they required and left a residue of those people to live. They soon began to intermarry with them and to participate in their worship of idols. Eventually they replaced the worship of Jehovah with the worship of Baal, the chief deity of those seven nations.

Isn't this the standard pattern of every new visitation of God? Supernatural power enables a group of committed ones to overcome the evil one and to conquer lost territory for the Church. The conquest never seems complete, and it isn't long before compromise and intermarriage begin to draw the people's hearts away from Christ Jesus. It is to be expected that they will turn to idolatry as others have done. The end will be slavery to the system instead of liberty in Christ Jesus.

Not only did Israel endure affliction from the hand of the LORD in a hundred different ways, but the nation was "delivered ... into the hands of the plunders." It is God's plan to punish the wicked by the wicked, and, accordingly, Israel experienced severe affliction during the siege of the Assyrians. When, after three years, King Shalmaneser finally conquered Israel, he transported nearly the entire nation into Assyria. Expatriation is an enormous trial. Israel's ruin involved the permanent loss of their national existence. More than two hundred years of idolatry and wickedness were followed by more than two thousand years of dispersion and alienation. Where are those ten tribes today?

Similarly, entire nations have gone into oblivion and large religious denominations have lost their identities after departing from the worship of Jehovah. Instead of worshiping the Lord God, they chose various forms of religious idolatry. When God cannot get a proper response with His afflictions, He turns us into the hands of plunderers — and their work is merciless, comprehensive and lasting. Many never come back to the worship of the Lord God. They have already been plundered and carried away captive. Their end is complete; they have collected their wages and "...the wages of sin is death" (Romans 6:23).

Is there no hope for those caught up in idolatry? There was none for Israel, but God extended mercy upon Judah for there were some distinct differences between the idolatry of Judah and that of Israel.

Little children, keep yourselves from idols. Amen (1 John 5:21).

Chapter 9

The Pattern of Judah's Idol Worship

God is just. This is not open for argument or even the expression of an opinion. God Himself declares: "...there is no other God besides Me, a just God and a Savior..." (Isaiah 45:21), and the New Testament calls Christ "The Holy One and the Just" (see Acts 3:14). Therefore, the tremendous difference between God's punishment of Israel and Judah for their respective idolatries can never be declared an injustice. God would have to violate His very nature to act unjustly.

God is a master at making the punishment fit the sin. Jesus alluded to this in His parabolic contrast of the faithful and the unjust servants. Jesus ended the story by saying:

> *And that servant who knew his master's will, and did not prepare himself or do according to his will, shall be beaten with many stripes. But he who did not know, yet committed things worthy of stripes, shall be beaten with few. For everyone to whom much is given, from him much*

will be required; and to whom much has been committed, of him they will ask the more (Luke 12:47-48).

Judah's seventy years in captivity for her idolatry stand in marked contrast to the permanent loss of identity imposed upon Israel. Because of the constancy of God, the difference must lie in the nature of the sinning of the two nations.

Judah's relationship to Israel

For many hundreds of years, the term "Israel" applied to all God's covenant people who came from the lineage of Abraham. That one family became a united nation under the leadership of Moses, Joshua and later David. After the death of David's successor, Solomon, the people asked their new king, Rehoboam, to lighten the burden of taxation that Solomon had imposed. After counseling with the young men at court, Rehoboam told the elders of Israel that his little finger was thicker than his father's loins. He would escalate their burdens — not diminish them. The king's harsh attitude split his kingdom. The ten northern tribes seceded and formed the nation of Israel under Jeroboam. This left Rehoboam the single tribe of Judah to move from the status of a mere tribe to the standing of a sovereign nation. While attempting to enforce authority, the king totally lost it. Like many pastors since his day, Rehoboam learned that a leader never has more authority than is granted to him by the people. Judah retained the holy city, the sacred Temple, and the consecrated priesthood. Judah's worship of Jehovah continued after the split in the kingdom. That was not true of Israel. Jeroboam substituted the golden calves in Bethel and Dan for Jerusalem's Temple and offered the priesthood to anyone willing to pay for it. The founding king wrote new laws and chose different feast days. Israel remained religious, but she departed from divine revelation. Jeroboam patterned everything according to the people's past religious patterns, but he allowed sufficient differences to separate the northern kingdom from the southern kingdom.

Jeroboam strengthened and perpetuated his political position by those religious differences. His idolatry successfully separated Israel from Judah forever. Even after the death of Rehoboam, those two would never again become one. Though related by blood, with a common heritage and similar pursuits in life, Israel's departure from the revealed worship of Jehovah formed an impenetrable barrier to unity. The golden calves insured the individuality of Israel.

God continued to deal with each nation separately. He sent prophets to both kingdoms. The same prophet often spoke to both Judah and Israel, but the responses were different. There were several spiritual reforms in Judah, and idols were often destroyed, but there was never such a reform in Israel — the golden calves were never tumbled. The idolatry Jeroboam began escalated progressively with little or no hindrance. Accordingly, Israel went into gross idolatry far ahead of Judah. Consistently, God used Israel as an illustration to Judah, warning the smaller nation to learn from the power of a bad example. Sometimes they responded positively; other times, they resisted God's lesson.

Many Bible teachers view Israel as an example of the false church and Judah as a pattern of the true Church. The false church is frequently the largest, the seemingly more profitable, and the one to show significant growth. Sidestepping the laws of God and substituting objects of worship harmonious with the daily lives of the people make their form of religion more popular.

I have frequently told ministerial groups: "If you really want the church to grow rapidly, do not let God get involved." God often slows down church growth because He is not merely interested in wood; His investment is in fruit. Great gardener that He is, He keeps pruning the wood back to force the production of fruit. He will, of course, have structure, but He develops it slowly.

Democracy in church government is embraced because it enables a congregation to sidestep the Bible and develop its own rules, laws and leadership. The ballot box allows leaders to do things in a way that is harmonious with the people's will. The issue ceases to be "What does God say?" and becomes "What do the people want?" Whenever we do things the way people want them done, we can easily draw people. The separation of one nation into Israel and Judah is as prevalent today as it was in the days of Rehoboam and Jeroboam. Some believers abide by God's laws and ways, while others devise their own religious codes of conduct.

Judah embraces Israel's law

The sacred historian reports of Judah: "Also Judah did not keep the commandments of the LORD their God, but walked in the statutes of Israel which they made" (2 Kings 17:19). God gave these commandments to Moses on Mt. Sinai through the mediacy of angels. The finger of God carved the first Ten Commandments on two tables of stone. Judah could not deny God's involvement in giving them the Law. Time proved that this, indeed, was God's Word to His people. It was a covenant agreement between God and His chosen people, and God never violated His part of the covenant. The prophets regularly reaffirmed these covenant laws, and every spiritual renewal revived them.

The charge is not that Judah did not know those commandments, they simply did not keep them. Many generations later, Jesus told His disciples: "If you know these things, happy are you if you do them" (John 13:17). God still looks for persons who *keep* His commandments. Many persons will preach God's Word, and even more will listen to that preaching, but hearing and knowing must be followed by doing. The Bible declares: "... be doers of the word, and not hearers only, deceiving yourselves" (James 1:22). I have often said that God has read none of the twenty-seven books I have written, but He watches every detail of my life. God is watching our lives more than He listens to our lips, and so is the world. It's about time we "walk our talk."

Judah kept God's religious rituals, but she would not keep God's written Word. That nation later discovered that the step of forsaking God's written Word was the turning point from their worship of Jehovah to their worship of idols. Modern Christians need to realize that we are already on the road to idol worship when we cease obeying the Word of God. Our disobedience to God demonstrates that we have already accepted another's will as the guiding force for our lives.

Refusal to obey God's commandments was bad enough, but Judah also "... walked in the statutes of Israel which they made" (2 Kings 17:19). Judah turned from divinely inspired commands to Israel's contrived codes, and so does the modern Church. Bylaws are more important than God's word to many Christians. What man says takes precedence over what God said. Today's Church rests upon ceremony, history and the perpetuation of the way we have always done things. Even when God speaks, we seldom hear and obey Him, especially if what He says conflicts with what key religious persons are saying.

Judah's deliberate embracing of the statutes of Israel was a radical turn from revelation to religion. The results were predictable. Although even a casual observance of Israel should have revealed the results of her codes, Judah followed those statutes because they appeared to be more convenient than God's law. The result was disaster. Surely if we see where a path leads and do not like its end, we are wise enough to choose another path, or are we? Judah wasn't. Mercifully, God let Israel be a demonstration to Judah, but Judah followed the same path and ended in the same place.

Somehow, what man devises seems better to us than what God has declared. Perhaps it is because man deals with the present, while God views our future end. Man writes for time, but God writes for eternity. Our present religious codes now permit us to do some things that God has forbidden. In the expediency of the hour, man says, "Go ahead. Do it." This appeals to our carnal natures but violates the spiritual laws God has established for our eternal well-being. Judah traded the eternal for the temporal. How easily the modern Church follows her example.

Judah flirts with Israel's lusts

Refusal to learn by observation forces us to learn from experience. Judah did not learn from Israel's example. God said through the prophet Jeremiah:

> *And I said, after she had done all these things, "Return to Me." But she did not return. And her treacherous sister Judah saw it. Then I saw that for all the causes for which backsliding Israel had committed adultery, I had put her away and given her a certificate of divorce; yet her treacherous sister Judah did not fear, but went and played the harlot also* (Jeremiah 3:7-8).

The elders of Judah consistently argued with Jeremiah that the presence of the Temple in the city of

Jerusalem would make them immune to captivity. They expressed the view that their involvement with the Temple, the priesthood and the rituals given to Moses made them an exception to the restrictions of God's Word. They discovered too late that they were wrong.

Presently there is an abundance of loose living in key religious leadership. On a few occasions, I've put my finger on a sin in such a leader's life. Instead of a repentant confession, the leaders have said, "I travel widely and have given myself totally to the Lord. God has made an exception for me." They seem to make a good case for themselves until I take them back to the cross of Christ and remind them that God didn't make an exception for "His only begotten Son" when He vicariously bore the sins of the world. If God turned His face from His Son, what grounds have we to believe that we can sin with immunity from punishment? There are no exceptions to the commands of God's Word, no matter how deeply involved we may be in the work of the Lord.

Today's Church may have the world's best praisers [Judah means *praise*], and we may develop the finest worship liturgy, but we do well to see what happened to those who came before us. We are not the first to discover public worship of God. Why did it cease? What were the steps of departure from a vital relationship with the Father? There is a strong hunger for another move of God. Why? Because the last move went into idolatry and prostituted itself. It moved from being centered on God to being centered on man. It produced kingdom builders who gathered people unto themselves. This century has experienced two or three major moves of God, and yet the Church is now praying for a fourth. How many groups of people will God have to energize before He gets someone who will obey Him? How long will it be before God finds people who will walk with Him? God yearns for someone He can trust, people He can give giftings to without them grandstanding the gift or building a kingdom on it. Somehow today's Church learns no more from observing the failure of others than Judah learned from Israel.

God severely judged Israel as an ongoing example for Judah. We are all aware of the recent public disclosures of immorality and greed in popular church leaders. God frequently chastens an individual publicly as a warning to others. God wants obedience, not devastation.

Judah had no intention of abandoning God to embrace the golden calves of Israel. That titillation of idolatry merely flirted with the pleasurable aspects of Israel's form of worship. How desperately Christians need to learn that casual lust for the things of the world is flirting with disaster. When the eyes wander, the heart soon follows. What starts as casual sin soon becomes chronic. Cursory lust soon controls us. Flirting with the thing that destroyed others is evidence of a death wish.

Judah follows Israel's idolatry

Flirtation may seem safe enough, but fascination with the forbidden eventually erupts into participation in the prohibited. Judah flirted with Israel's idolatry, for whatever reasons we may imagine, and eventually followed the idolatrous ways of that northern kingdom. Although Judah's involvement was progressive, the Bible especially condemns the overt acts of King Manasseh. His 55-year reign lowered Judah into such depths of idolatry that in spite of a subsequent revival under Josiah, the nation never completely returned to the worship of Jehovah.

Of the king, Manasseh, we read: " ... Manasseh seduced them to do more evil than the nations whom the LORD had destroyed before the children of Israel"

(2 Kings 21:9). What degeneracy. God was moved to such anger as to declare:

> *Because Manasseh king of Judah has done these abominations (he has acted more wickedly than all the Amorites who were before him, and has also made Judah sin with his idols), therefore thus says the LORD God of Israel: "Behold, I am bringing such calamity upon Jerusalem and Judah, that whoever hears of it, both his ears will tingle"* (2 Kings 21:11-12).

When God spoke through Jeremiah of the impending captivity of Judah, He said:

> *"And I will appoint over them four forms of destruction," says the LORD: "the sword to slay, the dogs to drag, the birds of the heavens and the beasts of the earth to devour and destroy. I will hand them over to trouble, to all kingdoms of the earth, because of Manasseh the son of Hezekiah, king of Judah, for what he did in Jerusalem"* (Jeremiah 15:3-4).

No subsequent acts ever atoned for the sins of Manasseh. No prophetic prayer or priestly ritual propitiated God. Even the zealous revival under Josiah could not dissuade God from pouring extreme judgment upon an entire nation because of the actions of Manasseh. Why? Because Manasseh brought extreme idolatry into the nation, and nothing done subsequently ever eradicated the propensity to worship at altars for sinning.

The specific actions of Manasseh are recorded in Second Kings, chapter 21. His embracing of what God had ordered destroyed was the first indictment against him: "And he did evil in the sight of the Lord, according to the abominations of the nations whom the LORD had cast out before the children of Israel" (2 Kings 21:2). He caused Judah to return to the religious practices that had so angered God as to cause Him to destroy seven nations that were mightier than the children of Israel (see Deuteronomy 7:1).

What is there that causes us to return to that which God has rejected? Church history shows that the reformation accepted by one generation is often abandoned by succeeding generations as they return to the practices that the reformers paid such a price to abandon. Perhaps the price of maintaining spiritual freedom seems too high to those who have received their liberty as a gift from their parents. On the other hand, it may simply be that our carnal nature prefers things our way instead of God's way. The second charge levied against Manasseh was the undoing of the reforms begun by Hezekiah:

> *For he rebuilt the high places which Hezekiah his father had destroyed; he raised up altars for Baal, and made a wooden image, as Ahab the king of Israel, had done; and he worshiped all the host of heaven and served them* (2 Kings 21:3).

How sad it is to see the continuing cycle of bondage/liberty in the Church of the living God. No wonder, then, that Paul admonished us: "As you have therefore received Christ Jesus the Lord, so walk in Him" (Colossians 2:6). Manasseh refused to walk in the spiritual reforms of his father, Hezekiah, and far too often that is true of the generation that follows a major revival. It seems easier to return to the former ways than to traverse new territory with Christ Jesus.

Hezekiah actively undid the reforms of his father. "He raised up altars for Baal" making it unnecessary for his people to go to the land of Israel to worship Baal. He also "made a wooden image" to Ashera and "worshiped all the host of heaven and served them." While this was, indeed, a return to the worship of the seven nations that had inhabited the Promised Land before Joshua's conquest, it is improbable that Manasseh was as conversant with their worship as he was with Israel's worship of those idol gods. He did not need to be a historian to uncover those forms of worship. His sister nation to the north did his research for him and demonstrated all forms of Baal worship. Manasseh simply copied in Judah the worship of Israel. It was politically unwise to replace the distinctive worship of Jehovah with its Temple and priesthood, so Manasseh cleverly added Baal worship to the worship of Jehovah. The historian says:

> *He also built altars in the house of the LORD, of which the LORD had said, "In Jerusalem I will put My name." And he built altars for all the host of heaven in the two courts of the house of the LORD ... He even set a carved image of Asherah that he had made, in the house of which the LORD had said to David and to Solomon his son, "In this house and in Jerusalem, which I have chosen out of all the tribes of Israel, I will put My name forever"* (2 Kings 21:4-5,7).

On the surface, it seems unthinkable that a king of Judah would so thoroughly desecrate the sacred Temple where God had sovereignly chosen to put His name and shekinah presence. But it was a deliberate and calculated move. Manasseh appeared pious by going to the Temple for worship. It was less offensive for the devout Jews to see their king at a foreign altar in the Temple than to see him in the house of Baal. Also, by bringing heathen altars and images into the holy place, it was easier to introduce idolatry to the people.

Fundamentally, Hezekiah worshiped in the right place. He merely worshiped the wrong gods. Satan has repeatedly used this deception throughout history. All too frequently, Christian missions have embraced pagan practices to get converts. Sometimes religion gives religious names to these customs, but the demonic forces behind them remain unchanged. Outwardly, it appears to be Christian, but in reality it is only paganism practiced in a different setting.

Recently a church on the eastern seaboard of the United States was desperate for a children's worker. They happily accepted the offer of a visitor to help them in this department. To their relief, she seemed very qualified to work with children, and the parents rejoiced at the reports that the children were speaking with tongues and were praying for each other — even laying hands on one another. The pastor joyfully reported to his congregation that great spiritual power was being released in the children's church. One suspicious elder decided to check it out for himself. What he saw horrified him. This woman was teaching the children how to use a mantra in transcendental meditation. It was true that great spiritual power was being released, but it was not divine power. The children were being taught to descend into the alpha state and to call up demons. The church was unable to recover from that experience and has since closed its doors.

If we build altars, we will have priests. Worldwide covens of witches fast and pray one day a week for the destruction of the Christian Church. They also have training schools to teach attractive women how to sexually seduce pastors in order to successfully expose them. Others are urged to volunteer for nursery work, so they can demonically influence the babies. The college graduates in these covens receive special instruction in working with young people, and then they go to churches, volunteering to become youth leaders. The enemy is content to reach for the coming generation while leaving the present generation of Christians alone. It is unfortunate that we often make it easy for them to reach their goals in our churches.

Like Manasseh, we allow heathen altars and images to be brought into the house of the Lord.

Once Manasseh made Judah comfortable with the addition of Baal worship to the worship of Jehovah, he dared to practice his worship more openly. We read: "Also he made his son pass through the fire, practiced soothsaying, used witchcraft, and consulted spiritists and mediums. He did much evil in the sight of the LORD, to provoke Him to anger" (2 Kings 21:6). When he went bad, he went all the way. There is no stopping point in practicing evil. The introductory excitement soon fades. Deeper and deeper depths of iniquity become necessary just to obtain the initial level of pleasure. The simple addition of a few non-Christian practices can eventually lead to extreme depths of spiritual depravity — such as happened to King Manasseh and his kingdom. It is unlikely that we will be an exception to the rule.

Judah experienced Israel's punishment

Judah became so involved with Israel's form of idolatry that the prophet declared:

> "For according to the number of your cities were your gods, O Judah; and according to the number of the streets of Jerusalem you have set up altars to that shameful thing, altars to burn incense to Baal" (Jeremiah 11:13).

The New International Version translates this: "You have as many gods as you have towns, O Judah."

Once we violate Jehovah's divine monopoly, there is no end to the multiplicity of gods that find their way into our lives. On occasion I have been so blessed with the presence of God in a local congregation that I am determined to return there. Sometimes the second visit is a bitter disappointment: After three years I cannot find the presence of God in their midst. Substitute gods are receiving the glory. Doctrine, pastor, buildings, pride or success have become the objects of adulation. The songs are the same and the ritual seems unchanged, but the object of their worship is no longer Jehovah God.

Whenever we build an altar to any other than Jehovah, we can be assured of worshipers at that altar. It is unfortunate that the human heart has an amazing propensity to embrace something short of God. We love our heros, even our religious heroes, and we find it difficult to deny our heroes the status of divinity. But we need to remember that all worship at altars for sinning brings the wrath of Jehovah upon us.

God warned Judah of unprecedented calamity: "Therefore thus says the LORD God of Israel: 'Behold, I am bringing such calamity upon Jerusalem and Judah, that whoever hears of it, both his ears will tingle' " (2 Kings 21:12). Judah refused to believe the prophetic warning, for they declared the presence of the Temple was their protection. They didn't realize that the desecration of the Temple and the forsaking of the God of the Temple was the root cause for the prophesied destruction. Judah had watched Israel go into captivity because of her idolatry, but that did not prevent her from embracing the very same idolatrous practices. They were to learn that to commit her sins is to receive her judgment.

God was not acting emotionally. He judged Judah carefully before pronouncing judgment upon the nation. He said: "And I will stretch over Jerusalem the measuring line of Samaria and the plummet of the house of Ahab; I will wipe Jerusalem as one wipes a dish, wiping it and turning it upside down" (2 Kings 21:13). God's first image is from the tools of the carpenter trade. With the use of a plummet line, builders determine if a wall is vertically straight or if it has the characteristics of the leaning tower of Pisa. When God said He would use the same plummet line on Judah that He had used on Israel, He was affirming that His judgment of Judah was no different than His judgment of Israel. God measured the same sin by the same standard, and it received the same judgment. Past righteousness does not cause God to overlook present unrighteousness.

So that everyone would understand the thoroughness of His examination, God also compared His action to wiping a dish — turning it over to better see both surfaces. God looks inward and outward. He examines the actions and the motives. He measures the power of the enemy who is pushing us into idolatry against the energy of His Spirit within us to keep us from false worship. No matter where God looks, we end up judged, for there is no acceptable excuse for worshiping at false altars — especially in God's house.

Because of what God found when He examined Judah, He declared, "So I will forsake the remnant of My inheritance and deliver them into the hand of their enemies ..." (2 Kings 21:14) God had delivered Judah from the hands of her enemies for many generations. Now He was about to deliver them to their enemies. Just as God's protection had been absolute, so was His impending judgment. The idolatry that had turned Judah away from God caused God to turn against her.

Similarly, our idolatry today will also turn God away from us. If we choose to serve the god of lust, Jehovah God may well abandon us to our lust. Then we'll find that enemy everywhere we turn — in the home, on the job, even in the church. Few things are more tragic than to have God deliver us to what we want. Paul said of a different generation:

[They] *changed the glory of the incorruptible God into an image made like corruptible man — and birds and four-footed beasts and creeping things. Therefore God also gave them up to uncleanness, in the lusts of their hearts, to dishonor their*

> *bodies among themselves, who exchanged the truth of God for the lie, and worshiped and served the creature rather than the Creator, who is blessed forever. Amen* (Romans 1:23-25).

God further said that Judah would "... become victims of plunder to all their enemies" (2 Kings 21:14). Judah learned too late what we need to know now. Bringing altars to sin into God's temple ends in subtraction rather than addition. Worship of multiple gods does not bring multiple blessings. Instead, it brings divine curses. Judah's punishment for following Israel into idolatry was both progressive and cumulative. By God's action, they lost their *peace* through calamity. They lost their *position* by being measured and wiped. They lost God's *presence* when He gave them to the enemy, and they lost their *possessions* to the repeated plunder of the enemy. They could have spared themselves if they had learned from observing their neighbors.

Little children, keep yourselves from idols. Amen (1 John 5:21).

Chapter 10

The Prophetic Anger Against Idolatry

Most people are more interested in what a prophet knows about the future than what he knows about God. Because of this, many read and even study the prophetic books of the Old Testament without gleaning the revelation of Jehovah these books contain. God does not reveal Himself as a prime cause or as the Supreme Being, although, of course, He is this and far more. God reveals Himself as a person with all the personality attributes. This concept is an accommodation to our inability to grasp a higher revelation. The purpose of the Bible is to introduce us to a personal God. God's most powerful self-revelation occurred when "... the Word became flesh and dwelt among us, and we beheld His glory, the glory as of the only begotten of the Father, full of grace and truth" (John 1:14).

God communicates with mankind as a person — not as an impersonal lawgiver. When we read the words that God speaks without picturing the One speaking, we miss much of the message He seeks to communicate. We fail to feel the heart of God when He speaks and consequently miss the love and concern in the voice of the Lord. We read of the severe punishments of God without being aware of the sensitive pathos God experiences when chastening His chosen people.

While ministering in a convention in Pittsburgh, I remarked how deeply I loved the Old Testament. A dear sister in the Lord came to me after that session and said: "I do not love the Old Testament," she said. "I am deathly afraid of it. Please pray for me." I think she verbalized the feelings of many Christians who see the judgments of God without seeing His justice. They read of His wrath without understanding His ways. It is not the Old Testament they fear, it is the picture of God that the Old Testament paints. They fail to balance the revelation of the holiness of God with the demonstration of His grace given in the New Testament.

For most of us, it is painful to admit that God is capable of hate. We've lived on a religious diet that forbids hatred and extols love. When we read of God hating, it seems to violate the very nature of God, which is love. Still, the Bible not only speaks of God hating, it requires us to join Him in that hatred. The psalmist said, "You who love the LORD: hate evil!" (Psalm 97:10) Love and hate are the opposing poles of life. As we learn to love what God loves, we need also to learn to hate what God hates. Conversely, when we reverse the polarity of our lives, we will begin to love what God hates and cease loving what God loves.

It is the nature of God to hate, and He especially hates idolatry. He metes out His greatest punishment on all ramifications of idolatry. God's anger with idolatry is not that it makes Him jealous, although the Scripture does say He is a jealous God. God is not insecure in His relationship with us. He does not need to react jealously for fear of losing us, for with the Word of His mouth He can create ten million more persons better than we. God is furiously jealous for the good of His covenant persons who have become the objects of His love. He responds in righteous anger to anything or anyone that limits, defiles or deforms those for whom He died. We need to realize that our greatest defense is God's jealous anger. He is against anything that would destroy us, and idolatry in any form has built-in destruction.

This divine anger can be heard in the voice of the prophets. God said to Jeremiah, "Therefore thus says the Lord God: 'Behold, My anger and My fury will be poured out on this place ...' " (Jeremiah 7:20) The terrible destruction of the Babylonian army, for which God claimed to be responsible, proved just how angry God had become. Unable to pull His people away from idolatry, He pulled them from their land and sent them into Babylon. That action was not the result of frustration. It was an exhibition of anger.

God hates the futility of idols

God holds a monopoly on divinity. He testifies: "... there is no other God besides Me, a just God and a Savior; there is none besides Me" (Isaiah 45:21). All idolaters worship false gods, whether the image they venerate is physical or psychological. Having warned Judah to refuse to learn the religious ways of the Gentiles and to ignore "the signs of heaven," God said:

For the customs of the peoples are futile; for one cuts a tree from the forest, the work of the hands of the workman, with the ax. They decorate it with silver and gold; they fasten it with nails and hammers so that it will not topple. They are upright, like a palm tree, and they cannot speak; they must be carried, because they cannot go by themselves. Do not be afraid of them, for they cannot do evil, nor can they do any good (Jeremiah 10:3-5).

Like a parent watching a small child treat a stuffed animal as though it were a living person, God watches us project life and personality into inanimate objects. If it was only child's play, God would be amused, but we are adults pretending to have contact with the Almighty, and our actions reflect a serious delusion. It is a lesson in futility for the idolater. For God, it is cause for anger. God asks through Isaiah:

> To whom will you liken Me, and make Me equal and compare Me, that we should be alike? They lavish gold out of the bag, and weigh silver in the balance; they hire a goldsmith, and he makes it a god; they prostrate themselves, yes, they worship. They bear it on the shoulder, they carry it and set it in its place, and it stands; from its place it shall not move. Though one cries out to it, yet it cannot answer nor save him out of his trouble (Isaiah 46:5-7).

God hates to see His people caught up in worship that is absolutely barren, empty and useless.

God presents idolatry as not only futile, but as a fraud. As the first stages of God's judgment came upon Judah, God confronted her:

> Stand now with your enchantments and the multitude of your sorceries, in which you have labored from your youth — perhaps you will be able to profit, perhaps you will prevail. You are wearied in the multitude of your counsels; let now the astrologers, the stargazers, and the monthly prognosticators stand up and save you from these things that shall come upon you. Behold, they shall be as stubble, the fire shall burn them; they shall not deliver themselves from the power of the

flame; it shall not be a coal to be warmed by, nor a fire to sit before! (Isaiah 47:12-14)

God challenged His people to recognize that the idolatry of the nations surrounding them was pure fraud. The very idols they worshiped could not even save themselves from the fire. God, who is truth, cannot stand the deception of a fraud.

One wonders how enlightened men and women could ever fall for the deception of idolatry. Like all frauds, idolatry presents itself in a beautiful package that promises far more than can ever be realized. Idols are money-makers for the artisans and priests. The idol makers of Ephesus sought to kill Paul for disturbing their business through the preaching of the gospel of the one true God. Even today idol makers carefully guard the source of revenue that idolatry brings to them. I have seen poor peasants pass the only piece of money they owned to the priest of the idol they sought to worship. I have seen the same thing done through Christian television. Widows and retired persons who live on fixed incomes have deprived themselves of necessities to contribute to the high lifestyle of a religious idol, or the high priest of that idol. Occasionally a local church suffers from similar treatment because of someone the congregation has set up as their idol.

Religious idols make money for the artisans and the priests, but they make misery for the worshipers because they are empty and fraudulent. When there is a genuine need for God, those worshipers discover that the object they have worshiped and supported is a hollow creation totally incapable of responding to them. When such revelation becomes a reality, resentment builds to high level anger, and we begin to realize why God was so angry with idolatry all along.

To God, idolatry is more than empty and fraudulent. God also views idolatry as provoking. He declared through the prophet:

> *"I have stretched out My hands all day long to a rebellious people, who walk in a way that is not good, according to their own thoughts; a people who provoke Me to anger continually to My face; who sacrifice in gardens, and burn incense on altars of brick; who sit among the graves, and spend the night in the tombs; who eat swine's flesh, and the broth of abominable things is in their vessels; who say, 'Keep to yourself, do not come near me, for I am holier than you!' These are smoke in My nostrils, a fire that burns all the day. Behold, it is written before Me: I will not keep silence, but will repay; even repay into their bosom — your iniquities and the iniquities of your fathers together,"* says the LORD, *"Who have burned incense on the mountains and blasphemed Me on the hills; therefore I will measure their former work into their bosom"* (Isaiah 65:2-7).

It doesn't take a second reading to realize that God is provoked. He compares His irritation with the smoke of an open fire in the nose and eyes.

Maturity brings an understanding of the danger in provoking another person too far. The married couple quickly learns the push point of their mates. There are certain gestures and voice intonations that clearly signal a warning that patience has been stretched to the breaking point. God was communicating that to Judah through the prophets, and He is still warning us that idolatry provokes Him, no matter how we may package it.

God hates what idols represent

Oh how we love what we can produce. Look at the self-sacrificing love that parents lavish on the child they created through their union. We brag about our accomplishments and attainments, and horde our possessions. This has merit unless it becomes an extreme obsession. When we begin to ascribe divine attributes to the work of our hands, we incur God's hatred. No matter how we may view our idols, God sees them for what they really are:

> *Their idols are silver and gold, the work of men's hands. They have mouths, but they do not speak; eyes they have, but they do not see; they have ears, but they do not hear; noses they have, but they do not smell; they have hands, but they do not handle; feet they have, but they do not walk; nor do they mutter through their throat. Those who make them are like them; so is everyone who trusts in them* (Psalm 115:4-8).

Twentieth-century religious idols are equally reprehensible to God. In a conference at which I was speaking on this subject, I asked the conferees to call out modern idols. Their responses were incisive. They saw modern Christians worshiping at the altars of buildings, doctrines, ritual and structure. They said that possessions, positions, sexuality, music, art, education, science, athletics and many other "innocent" things now occupy a place in many lives that belongs to God. Obviously, what is an idol to one person may not even come close to being an idol to another, for it is not the image, but the attitude of the heart, that makes an idolater out of any of us.

Everything on this list are the creation of men and women, but they often receive the adulation and reverence that is due to God alone. Many Christians spend more time being involved with these than with the Lord. The entire structure of their life revolves around one or more of these "idols."

An obvious illustration of this is modern television. The church used to be the center of community life and all social activities centered around it. Not any more. Television is now the focal point in the lives of most members in our communities. The church often finds it convenient to schedule its services and activities to fit around television specials. A pastor told me that he brought a television set to church, placed it on the communion table and turned it on so all in the auditorium could keep track of a televised event during the sermon. He kept the attendance figure high, but what did the congregation worship during the service? It is unlikely that the focus of the people remained on God.

The New Testament extends idolatry to cover anything that replaces devotion to God. Marital love is not idolatry, but it is possible to make an idol out of one's mate. Money is a useful medium of exchange that is not immoral in nature, but it is possible to become so obsessed with a love for money that the obsession leads to idolatry. We do well to ask ourselves whether our dependance is upon our monetary system or upon the Lord Jesus Christ. At whatever point we amass enough money that we no longer feel our need of God, we have created an idol.

God hates what idols represent — dependence upon something short of God. Even spiritual things can be turned into idols. "My ministry," "my church," "my giftings" — all evidence an obsession with self that has the potential for idolatry in it. Any ministry that repeatedly calls attention to something short of God has at least entered the fringes of idolatry. How easy it is to be sucked into the vortex of idolatry once our gaze shifts from God to anything less.

God's hatred of idols escalates when idols become an "incarnation" of satan. Behind idols are demon spirits. All ancient cultures considered their idols as visual representations of their invisible gods. The Bible suggests that demon forces often took advantage of that belief. Paul wrote:

> *But I say that the things which the Gentiles sacrifice they sacrifice to demons and not to God, and I do not want you to have fellowship with demons. You cannot drink the cup of the Lord and the cup of demons; you cannot partake of the Lord's table and of the table of demons* (1 Corinthians 10:20-21).

Both God and satan have given themselves a visible form to initiate faith. God comes in the person of Jesus; satan comes concealed as an idol. Jesus comes "full of grace and truth," while satan comes full of fear and deception. Christ came to restore; satan came to destroy. Each represents a spirit realm. Each desires our worship. Idols are a substitute for God. Idolatry is a perversion of and a turning away from the knowledge of the true God. Paul called idolatry a work of the flesh (see Galatians 5:19-20) and warned Christians to shun the worship of idols: "Therefore, my beloved, flee from idolatry" (1 Corinthians 10:14). Idols claim to do what God has already done for us, and they receive gifts and adulation that belong entirely to God.

Idolatry is a substitute for God, and God has always hated substitutes. God may bless supplements, but He always curses substitutes. Idolatry substitutes the creature for the Creator, fear for faith, and a religion of darkness for a revelation of divine light. Those who worship idols trade a religious experience for relationship with God, and they substitute demons for God. Any time we allow a substitute for God into our lives, we will face His jealous anger.

God hates what idols do to worshipers

Idolatry not only builds altars for sinning, it alters the life of the idolater. This is probably the greatest cause for God's hatred of idolatry. Just as there are times when parents must firmly resist their children's desire to participate in an activity that the parents know will be destructive to the children, so God rises in strength to resist our participation in idol worship. He knows the potential of destruction that is involved.

The first action of idolatry is to prostitute our worship, for idolatry inexorably associates itself with worship. We realize that worship is an instinct with which we are born. We must worship something to survive. The only area of choice is the object of our worship — and idolatry offers an object much lower than God. While altars for sinning may fulfill our urge to worship, they can never give us the benefits of true worship, for all idolatry cuts us off from God rather than bringing us into His presence.

Worship is an expression of wonder, awe or fear — often of the unknown. This explains why some persons worship fire, the stars, the sun, storms, volcanos, etc. Worship is an individual's attempt to respond to an object that generates deep admiration. We worship the "thing" because we don't know the unknown that is behind it. Idolatry capitalizes on our ignorance and offers us a visual form that becomes a representation of the invisible God. When God gave the Ten Commandments, He expressly prohibited any representation of Himself in tangible form (see Exodus 20:4). The Old Testament prophets repeated this message. Every violation of that commandment led to idolatry.

God hates idolatry not only because it gives a visual representation of the invisible God, but also because it localizes the omnipresent God. Although that is very satisfactory to human nature, it is an affront to the divine nature that can neither be visualized nor localized. Just as Aaron did not present the golden calf as a replacement for God, so those who have their icons and statues as part of their worship explain to us that they are not idols — they are merely visual aids to faith. Yet Aaron's calf became an idol that replaced Jehovah, and Moses' brazen serpent became an object of worship for later generations. The human heart today is no different.

If I place a horny toad in front of you to help you respond to God, and say: "This is your God," it won't be long before God and horny toads will be the same thing in your mind. Any adoration that proceeds from you will go to the horny toad. This is the curse of idolatry. We need to be consistently on guard against visualization — even in prayer — for there is little distinction between a mental image and a metal image. Whenever we use visualization, we walk in the danger of worshiping the image.

Idolatry is the fruit of disobedience. Through the message of the prophets it is easy to hear God's anger that is aroused by disobedience. God said through Jeremiah:

> *"For I earnestly exhorted your fathers in the day that I brought them up out of the land of Egypt, until this day, rising early and exhorting, saying, 'Obey My voice.' Yet they did not obey or incline their ear, but everyone walked in the imagination of his evil heart; ... and they have gone after other gods to serve them; the house of Israel and the house of Judah have broken My covenant which I made with their fathers." Therefore thus says the LORD: "Behold, I will surely bring calamity on them which they will not be able to escape; and though they cry out to Me, I will not listen to them. Then the cities of Judah and the inhabitants of Jerusalem will go and cry out to the gods to whom they offer incense, but they will not save them at all in the time of their trouble"* (Jeremiah 11:7,8,10-12).

The breaking of God's covenant and their refusal to obey God's voice opened both Israel and Judah to idolatry. God said in anger that they would have to turn to those idols for help in time of trouble, but, of course, no help would be available.

Paul was well aware of the connection between disobedience and idolatry, for he wrote: "... you once walked according to the course of this world, according to the prince of the power of the air, the spirit who now works in the sons of disobedience" (Ephesians 2:2). The declaration is obvious: Satan works in disobedient lives. This principle is true of individuals as well as groups of persons. The congregation that deliberately disobeys what God is saying opens itself to the deceptive work of the enemy. Many churches that are earnestly praying for revival will not experience a move of God until those congregations begin to obey the last thing the Lord instructed them to do. The dryness and lack of the Spirit of God in their midst is not God's fault. Disobedience caused them to violate a covenant and opened them to satanic hindrance, if not direct satanic activity.

Acts of disobedience open us to the spirit of disobedience, and that spirit will create idolatry in our hearts. The object of worship we form is meaningless to the spirit of disobedience. It is fine with this spirit if we choose to carve an idol out of soap as the object of our worship, for he knows that he will ultimately be the recipient of that worship.

We need not travel to Third World nations to find idolatry. It is available in many churches of Western culture. The only difference is the object chosen for adoration. God said: "For rebellion is as the sin of witchcraft, and stubbornness is as iniquity and idolatry ..." (1 Samuel 15:23) When we become stubborn against God, we become our own god. We set our ways above His ways, thereby making ourselves the supreme being in our own little world.

Only a person who has never met God will take God's anger lightly. There is absolutely no limit to what God can do in venting His anger against idolatry. Israel was completely destroyed as a nation. God sent them into Assyrian captivity and never allowed them to return to their homeland. Ezekiel watched as God removed His glory from Judah in three stages. First God's glory lifted from the Holy Place and rested in the outer court of the Temple. From there it moved to the Mount of Olives, and later it was totally withdrawn into heaven — never to return. Jewish historians say that it was never again seen in the reconstructed Temple in Jerusalem. God's anger over Judah's idolatry was demonstrated in progressively severe measures. The first siege of Nebuchadnezzar brought famine and captivity to many. But that did not turn Judah from the worship of idols, so God sent the king of Babylon back to blockade Jerusalem from any contact with the outside world. The resulting famine induced severe pestilence and ended in the slaughter or captivity of all the inhabitants of the capitol city. Then the magnificent Temple was totally destroyed and Jerusalem was mercilessly torn apart. The tribe of Judah knew servitude in Babylon for seventy years. Most of the tribe never returned. God's anger was devastating and lengthy. Long before God actually punished His people, He warned them through the prophets; but they would not hear His words nor feel His hot displeasure. Consequently, they experienced divine wrath. God is long-suffering, but He is not indulgent. Once He begins to display His anger, it is devastating. Little wonder, then, that David cried: "O LORD, do not rebuke me in Your anger, nor chasten me in Your hot displeasure" (Psalm 6:1).

Idolatry obviously separates us from God's *presence*, but not from His *punishment*. Like Adam and Eve, we often choose knowledge over relationship and are driven from our spiritual gardens. Acting like Saul when he went to the witch at Endor, we frequently choose supernatural interventions over the voice of God, thereby losing the kingdom God had once entrusted to us. The convenience of the golden calves over the cost of God's presence may lead us to act like Jeroboam or a preference for earthly security instead of divine approval may entice us to walk in the paths of Ananias and Sapphira. Whatever our idol, it may cost us our lives. Our tendencies to give our personal desires and goals higher priorities than obedience to the Word and will of God causes God to vent His anger toward our idolatrous nature. God's anger may first be revealed through the angry words of prophets, but unless we repent and turn from our idolatry, we will find ourselves in the very hands of an angry God. The New Testament warns us, "Beware, brethren, lest there be in any of you an evil heart of unbelief in departing from the living God; ... it is a fearful thing to fall into the hands of the living God" (Hebrews 3:12; 10:31).

Perhaps we treat idolatry too lightly because we do not fully understand what idolatry really produces. Just as there is often a great difference between the picture in the seed catalogue and what the seed actually produces, so there is a disparity between the picture satan paints of idolatry and the actual product of that idolatry.

Little children, keep yourselves from idols. Amen (1 John 5:21).

Chapter 11

The Product of Worshiping Idols

A fundamental law of physics we learned in high school follows: "For each action there is an equal reaction." The premise being that if you do not want a reaction, prevent the initial action. Similarly, every farmer knows that the purpose of planting seed is to reap a harvest. If you don't want the crop, don't plant the seeds. It is not only in physics and agriculture that the law of cause and effect applies. Every area of life has established this principle. The Bible warns: "For as he thinks in his heart, so is he" (Proverbs 23:7). Concepts condition conduct as surely as action induces a reaction. This is why advertisers seek to produce positive impressions about their product. Sometimes they dedicate most of the ad to creating a "yes" attitude and mention the product only in the final few seconds as a tie in.

Paul warned believers:

Do not be deceived, God is not mocked; for whatever a man sows, that he will also reap. For he

> *who sows to his flesh will of the flesh reap cor-*
> *ruption, but he who sows to the Spirit will of the*
> *Spirit reap everlasting life* (Galatians 6:7-8).

This is not the law of divine retribution; it is the law of sowing and reaping. The product reaped will be consistent with the seed sown. If God should choose to sit idly by and ignore our idolatry, our very behavior would still produce spiritual destruction. Just as knowledge of the seed gives advanced information of the crop to be harvested, so the result of idolatry is predictable even before the idolatrous action begins. God seeks to warn us of this disastrous end with His great foreknowledge.

Idolatry destroys morality

In speaking to idolatrous Judah, Isaiah said, "But come here, you sons of the sorceress, you offspring of the adulterer and the harlot! ... [you who are] inflaming yourselves with gods under every green tree..." (Isaiah 57:3,5) Isaiah poetically declared that an early product of idolatry is destroyed morality. It is characteristic of idolatry that it becomes licentious. No idolatry lifts moral standards, for idolatry lacks power to boost a person to greater heights. It can merely accommodate the natural depravity of the human soul. As we have already seen, the idolatry of Bible times embraced prostitution as part of its ritual. That was among the attractions of Baal worship. The availability of male and female prostitutes and the religious approval of ritual promiscuity was attractive to the carnal lusting after strange flesh.

Sexual immorality has consistently been part of false worship, and sometimes it invades the true worship of God. We may rest assured that any time worship moves into the sexual realm, it has already ceased to be worship of the true and living God. Idolatry may ignite sexual passion in its worshipers, but God never inflames lust. Any testimonies of sexual encounters with God are erroneous. Such contact, if more than fantasy, was with impersonating demons.

God never violates us. He who consistently condemns lust, whether for things, positions, fame or sex, never expresses it toward us. He has given us love and passion, and He has also supplied proper channels for those drives to find satisfaction. God never creates an appetite unless He also supplies a satisfaction for that appetite. Conversely, the enemy loves to create appetites that cannot be satisfied, which is what Isaiah means by: "inflaming yourselves with gods under every green tree."

Sin constantly lowers the moral standards of an individual and of a nation. In writing to his spiritual son, Timothy, who was bishop over several churches, Paul warned:

> *But know this, that in the last days perilous times will come: For men will be lovers of themselves, lovers of money, boasters, proud, blasphemers, disobedient to parents, unthankful, unholy, unloving, unforgiving, slanderers, without self-control, brutal, despisers of good, traitors, headstrong, haughty, lovers of pleasure rather than lovers of God, having a form of godliness but denying its power. And from such people turn away! For of this sort are those who creep into households and make captives of gullible women loaded down with sins, led away by various lusts, always learning and never able to come to the knowledge of the truth* (2 Timothy 3:1-7).

This comprehensive list quite accurately defines the decadence of morals so characteristic of our day. Morality decays rapidly when we replace God with idols of any form.

The preaching of holiness and morality is uncommon in our generation. We have replaced it with situation ethics, the inherent power in the individual, and pop psychology. Unfortunately, when we get away from the moral teachings of the Word of God, we soon find ourselves energized to behave contrary to the standards God has set. As unpopular as it may be, we desperately need to be reminded that apart from God each of us is a putrid mess of immoral desires. No one has the inherent power to live righteous lives. God's Word clearly says, "There is none righteous, no, not one" (Romans 3:10). We need the righteousness that comes from Christ Jesus, but we will never find it at altars for sinning.

When idolatry replaces the worship of God, we experience a depreciation of moral standards in our lives, our homes, our churches and our nation. Even the mildest form of idolatry opens us to the captivity of the devil. Paul told Timothy:

> *...in humility correcting those who are in opposition, if God perhaps will grant them repentance, so that they may know the truth, and that they may come to their senses and escape the snare of the devil, having been taken captive by him to do his will* (2 Timothy 2:25-26).

Satan hooks persons with the bait of elementary idolatry, and then holds them captive to do his will. Once he sets his hook, the enemy often leaves the captured person alone until he needs him or her. A church may know peace until an insignificant issue arises; then persons come out of the woodwork to do battle and to oppose the pastor. Anger, malice, strife and selfishness remain hidden until the devil needs to use those forces. Then those persons in whom the negative moral attitudes are working find themselves at the disposal of the devil instead of the divine. The idol in their heart has energized them and the devil controls them.

How many persons find themselves slaves to controlling passions whether it be television, sports or sexual lusts? Their addiction is as real as that of the dope addict. In response to the pastor's Bible-reading program, they argue that they cannot find time to read the Bible through each year, which would require only 65 hours for an average reader. These same busy Christians spend a comparable amount of time each month enjoying one or more of their idols. The energy that binds them to their idols is not divine energy; it does nothing to elevate the moral standards of these captive slaves. Idolatry more than opposes morality — it destroys it.

Idolatry ridicules God

As Isaiah again addresses idolatrous Judah he asks: "Whom do you ridicule? Against whom do you make a wide mouth and stick out the tongue ...? (Isaiah 57:4) We might as well recognize that another product of altars of idolatry is the ridicule of God. The modern Church has an abundance of persons who mock God. They listen to the Word and respond with a loud "Amen!" but they walk out the door of the church and promptly ignore every precept they praised earlier.

Those who fix their affections on something short of God might consider God to be as some teenagers think of their parents — "old fogies." In their minds, the rules are restrictive, the advice is outdated and the standards are too victorian. Like the prodigal son, they act as though they have more wisdom than their parents, and they want to try it "my way." While reaching for their independence, they often heap ridicule on those who gave them existence, education and the leadership that has brought them to where they are in life.

Idolaters ridicule Jehovah God in speech, action and attitudes. Among the religious, it is not overtly directed against God. Instead they direct their ridicule at the pastor, the sermon, the church and other Christians in the congregation. How quickly they forget that Jesus said, "...inasmuch as you did it to one of the least of these My brethren, you did it to Me" (Matthew 25:40). The standard Sunday dinner for many Christians is roast preacher.

It is always interesting to me that overt satan-worshipers love to go out of their way to ridicule the true worship of God. They delight in obtaining communion elements in order to mock the death of Christ. They enjoy sneaking into church buildings to have sexual orgies. They will even deface and desecrate a religious cemetery, for mockery of God is at the heart of idolatry.

Idolaters set themselves up for retribution when they lower themselves to mock God, His ways, His works, His words and His workmen. The mocker of God reaps mockery by God. The wise man quoted God as saying, "I also will laugh at your calamity; I will mock when your terror comes" (Proverbs 1:26). Perhaps the old cliche should be recalled: "He who laughs last laughs best."

Idolatry is transgression of God's Word

In addition to the charge of mocking God, Isaiah 57:4 adds: "... Are you not children of transgression, offspring of falsehood...?" (Isaiah 57:4) Transgression is disobedience to the known will of God. Few modern Christians can claim ignorance of the will of God. We have Bibles, churches, pastors, Christian radio and television broadcasts, and close fellowship with other Christians. It is likely that we know the will of God, for it is the Father's responsibility to make that will known to His children. He has clearly expressed it in His Word, and He further quickens that will to the heart and mind of the true worshiper. Fundamentally, the will of God is to do the last thing He told us to until He tells us to do something else. Far too often we begin in obedience and taper off into disobedience.

When the devil tempted Jesus in the wilderness concerning worship, "Jesus said to him, 'Away with you, satan! For it is written, "You shall worship the LORD your God, and Him only you shall serve" ' " (Matthew 4:10). This is a direct quote from the Old Testament, which gives us a double witness. The principle contained herein is that adoring, submitting unduly, or exhibiting passion for anything short of God is idolatrous transgression. "You shall worship the LORD your God." God has a divine monopoly as the object of worship.The worship of any thing or any person other than God is a flagrant transgression of God's Word.

The worship of idols, in any form, is participation in the forbidden or the exchange of allegiance to God for allegiance to something short of God. Either way it is rebellious transgression. We need to remember that "The way of transgressors is hard" (Proverbs 13:15, KJV). Not only does the transgressor make life hard for himself, but the demons behind idolatry also make life difficult, as does God, Himself, who brings calamity on all transgressors.

When speaking of great judgments from God, the prophet Micah cried: "All this is for the transgression of Jacob and for the sins of the house of Israel. What is the transgression of Jacob? Is it not Samaria? And what are the high places of Judah? Are they not Jerusalem?" (Micah 1:5) God saw the golden calves of Israel and Judah's idol altars erected in Jerusalem as ultimate transgressions against Himself and His Word. God still views idolatry as an ultimate transgression. What a shame that the Church on earth participates in this while greatly condemning lesser sins of the flesh that God so quickly forgives and forgets. How great is our need to see through the eyes of God!

Idolatry invokes devastation

Still another product of altars for sinning is the combined devastation of the loss of God's presence and the perpetual churning of iniquity. God continued to cry to Judah through Isaiah saying:

> *For the iniquity of his covetousness I was angry and struck him; I hid and was angry, and he went on backsliding in the way of his heart. ... But the wicked are like the troubled sea, when it cannot rest, whose waters cast up mire and dirt. "There is no peace," says my God, "for the wicked"* (Isaiah 57:17,20-21).

For the person who has known the peace and pleasure of God's presence, the loss of His presence is absolutely devastating. It induces a desolation of spirit that is worse than the loneliness felt when partners in a loving marriage are separated by death. The spirit grieves with an inconsolable mourning that also affects the person's soul and body. For a season, at least, the person's whole being feels devastated.

But separation from God is not the only source of the devastation idolatry brings. Isaiah compares the restlessness of the idolater with a churning ocean. The iniquity of idolatry erodes the foundation of life like the churning waves of a stormy sea. It does not destroy everything with one action, but relentlessly washes away the very foundations of life, leaving ruin, devastation and destruction in its wake.

We should never allow ourselves to be deceived by what appears to be a beautiful side of evil. It is true that the devil has the power to appear as an angel of light for a short season, but it is a very brief period of radiance. Darkness, disease and death follow when his brief flame flickers out. Visit the hospitals and see the destruction that cigarettes, alcohol, venereal diseases and AIDS have inflicted upon his worshipers. Talk with inmates in one of our overcrowded prisons. They will tell you that although they were drawn by an evil attraction, they now live with the ugly side of that evil. There is no beauty left. Broken homes, ruined marriages and abused children give silent testimony to the devastation that comes from worshiping at altars for sinning. Idolatry is never constructive; it always destroys. Some devastation that churches encounter comes because of idolatry. God withdraws His presence when anything replaces Him as the focus of worship. This leaves the congregation vulnerable to the havoc that demonic forces can induce. Pride, power plays and politics quickly replace jubilant worship. Programs substitute for the divine presence, and dissatisfaction becomes the rule rather than the exception. Such was the lot of Israel after worshiping the golden calf, and it will be the fate of all Christian groups who build altars to sinning by substituting idols for Jehovah God.

Often the spirit of dissatisfaction induces a church split. I have observed that the dissenting group rarely grows and becomes productive unless the issue that produced the division is resolved, and forgiveness is sought and received. All avenues for enemy activity must be closed or the fledgling group of dissenters will not survive.

Similarly, individuals often seem unable to come into personal deliverance because in their past they submitted authority of their lives to demon powers by worshiping religious idols. Until they revoke that authority, there is little hope of victory no matter what else they do religiously. Satan will not give up territory over which he has legal authority, and idolatry grants him far more authority than we recognize. We must renounce idolatry if we expect satanic forces to respond to our commands.

Idolatry prostitutes worship

Perhaps the most obvious product of our altars for sinning is its prostitution of our worship. The force of idolatry is not directed at destroying worship, it merely seeks to pervert it. Worshiping at altars for sinning first degrades the worshiper, then it perverts the worship, and finally it demeans the One who should be worshiped. It desecrates a precious God-given drive.

In the passage from Isaiah that we have been looking at in this chapter, the prophet says of idol worshipers: "... [you have] debased yourself even to Sheol" (Isaiah 57:9). This is so characteristic of idol worshipers. Watch idolaters at worship. They crawl over stones on their knees and beat and cut their bodies. They withdraw from normal life and often fast to the point of emaciation. They offer their children as human sacrifices. They wail, moan, mutter and cry, but they never get a response from their god. The more desperate their need, the more they debase themselves or other worshipers.

Christians need to take care lest they fall into the same trap. The contrast between our level of righteousness and the righteousness of our holy God is so great that we often magnify our negatives rather than exalt God's positives. None of us has an inherent right to come into the presence of God, but God has mercifully conferred that privilege upon us. We have a right to worship because of His invitation, not because of our reputation.

Sometimes we think that verbally running down another person will make us look good — it doesn't. When we debase other Christians, we also debase ourselves. Satan loves to use a Christian to lower the reputation of another Christian, for he knows that debasing worshipers is a by-product of idolatry.

Christ came to *elevate* us, not to *depreciate* us. Wherever the gospel has been embraced, men and women have been lifted to higher levels of living. Dignity, not disgrace, is the gift of the gospel. Idolatry, in contrast, lowers men and women to the lowest possible level of life.

Not only does worshiping at altars of idolatry degrade the worshiper, but it perverts their worship. Ezekiel, the priest turned prophet, was among the first contingent of captives taken into Babylon. God repeatedly spoke to him declaring that Jerusalem would fall to King Nebuchadnezzar and the Temple would be destroyed. It was a difficult message to deliver, and even more difficult to believe. It seemed to violate everything Ezekiel had learned about the Holy City and its magnificent Temple to Jehovah. In the eighth chapter of his book, Ezekiel recounts how the Lord took him by a lock of his hair and transported him, in vision, back to Jerusalem to let him see what God saw. Although the sight broke Ezekiel's heart, it helped him understand why God so often called Judah "a rebellious house."

God first showed Ezekiel the true worship of the seventy elders of Judah. Ushered into the inner court where the glory of the Lord still resided, Ezekiel saw an idol image erected in the Holy of Holies. At God's command, Ezekiel dug a hole in the wall and discovered a door that led to a secret chamber. He said:

So I went in and saw, and there — every sort of creeping thing, abominable beasts, and all the idols of the house of Israel, portrayed all around on the walls. And there stood before them seventy men of the elders of the house of Israel, and in their midst stood Jaazaniah the son of Shaphan.

> *Each man had a censer in his hand, and a thick*
> *cloud of incense went up* (Ezekiel 8:10-11).

What an amazing perversion within the worship of Jehovah. The elders still met at the Temple, but they had a secret idol alongside the Ark of the Covenant and a secret room filled with the multiple idols Israel had worshiped before her captivity. The seventy men were not merely inspecting the idol images, they were actively worshiping them, as evidenced by the incense burners in their hands. Then Jehovah said to Ezekiel:

> *... Son of man, have you seen what the elders of*
> *the house of Israel do in the dark, every man in*
> *the room of his idols? For they say, "The LORD*
> *does not see us, the LORD has forsaken the land"*
> (Ezekiel 8:12).

That the elders had found substitute gods when they could no longer find the presence of Jehovah was bad enough, but the people of Judah were not far behind. Ezekiel reports:

> *So He brought me into the inner court of the Lord's*
> *house; and there, at the door of the temple of the*
> *LORD, between the porch and the altar, were*
> *about twenty-five men with their backs toward*
> *the temple of the LORD and their faces toward the*
> *east, and they were worshiping the sun toward*
> *the east* (Ezekiel 8:16).

The outer court where the priests offered sacrifices to Jehovah was now being used for sun worshipers. Although the men were in the proper place of worship, they were worshiping the wrong god. Even the women worshiped perversely. Ezekiel reports: "So He brought me to the door of the north gate of the Lord's house; and to my dismay, women were sitting there weeping for Tammuz" (Ezekiel 8:14). The women, the young men and the elders of Judah were worshiping, from outside the court all the way into the Holy of Holies, but all that worship was going to idol gods.

Once during a praise session in church, I dared to ask the Lord to show me who or what the people were worshiping. It so devastated me that I have not repeated that request. Some were worshiping their golf scores, others were worshiping their sex drives, a few were worshiping their lovers, many were worshiping themselves. Only a few in that congregation genuinely had Jehovah God on their minds as they participated in the praise ritual of that congregation. How easy it is to be in the right place doing the right thing, but directing it all to the wrong object. Idolatry cleverly prostitutes worship by directing it from the Lord who loves us and diverting it to an uncaring source.

Whenever the level of worship degrades the worshiper and perverts the worship by directing it to another, it demeans the One who should be worshiped. It projects a character to God that is far beneath the character He has revealed for Himself.

When Isaiah was talking about Judah's idolatry, he also said: "Among the smooth stones of the stream is your portion; they, they, are your lot! Even to them you have poured a drink offering, you have offered a grain offering. Should I receive comfort in these?" (Isaiah 57:6) Judah was substituting creation for the Creator, just as we so often do. The beauty of creation inspires awe and produces a soulish pleasure, but they should never prime us to worship the creation. The glory in creation should bring us to a knowledge of God. What prostitution it is for us to worship God's handiwork more than we worship the hand of God. It is easy for us to release our adoration toward God's performance instead of to His person, but God is never satisfied to have us worship what He has done over who He is.

There is nothing positive in idolatry. It gives us a negative concept of God and offers us a false hope. It degrades the worshiper and involves him in perverted worship. What little sensual pleasure may be realized in idolatry is more than offset by the shame, degradation, humiliation and needless sacrifice it induces. Idolatry is devilish in every form. We need deliverance from its power, its presence and the penalty it extracts from us. But how can we get out of this trap into which we have fallen? Does God have an answer for idolatry?

Little children, keep yourselves from idols. Amen (1 John 5:21).

Chapter 12

The Pulverizing of the Things We Adore

Adam and Eve responded to God with self-will, but it did not replace the worship of God in their lives. It is not until the second generation that we find such a clear distinction. By the time of Abraham, idolatry was far more prevalent than the worship of Jehovah. God called Abram, as he was known in Ur of Chaldea, and in obedience, that man of faith followed the leading of God into what would become the Promised Land. His forsaking of idolatry was complete, and the families that came from him never forsook the worship of Jehovah.

Even when the children of Israel were in idolatrous Egypt, the surrounding idolatry never replaced their worship of Jehovah. We read of some instances in which they sought to supplement their faith with physical objects, but their worship never involved the abandonment of God. Even the golden calf of Aaron was not originally intended to be a replacement of Jehovah.

Like all sin, the acceptance of idolatry often leads to an accommodation to it, which opens the door for embracing it in addition to the pure worship of Jehovah. It was not until the reign of Jeroboam that idolatry became rampant enough to replace the worship of Jehovah, and even that was a gradual process.

But that idolatry was not innocent just because it didn't supplant the worship of the true and living God. The smallest level of idolatry pollutes faith and paves the way for greater inroads by idolatry. The great danger in the modern Church is that we, like Judah, continue with all the correct outer forms while adding various forms of idolatry to our worship. Because we do not define the objects of our worship as idols, we comfortably put Christian names on them and add them to our worship rituals. The nations of Israel and Judah succumbed to idolatry, and so will we, unless we learn from their bad examples.

Although hundreds of years passed between the call of Abraham and the final embracing of idolatry by Judah, there is no period in Scripture when idolatry was totally absent. From the Garden of Eden to Christ's letters to the churches, idolatry has consistently mixed itself with pure worship. There is always the coexistence of the true Church and the false. Church history tells of periods when the idolatrous church forced the true Church to go underground. It also tells of other seasons when the true Church strongly contested the idolatrous practices of the false church. When God pours life into His body, the workings of death are broken up, just as a living seed can break through a concrete sidewalk.

Jesus graphically illustrated this mixture of the true and the false in His parable of the tares and wheat growing in the same field together. At harvest time, the angels were sent to gather the tares into bundles to be destroyed by burning. It is likely that we will have the idolatrous among us until the end of time when God's angels will gather idolaters into bundles to be reserved until the day of judgment.

Pulverizing idols is a personal task

Since the removal of the false from the world is an angelic task, there is little sense in setting ourselves up as reformers to change the world. Several kings of Judah instituted a return to pure worship and tore down the idols in the land, but their reforms were incomplete. Those revivals seldom lasted beyond the life span of the king as his successor often returned to the old ways.

This is not to make light of those reforms, for they delayed the degeneracy of the nation and were redemptive to a generation. Likewise, we may not be able to change the world, but we can change our own lives. We may not completely alter the future, but we can affect our present. Complete cleansing from idolatry in the modern Church may be beyond our faith levels, but we can cleanse our households from idols.

While we may argue that the prophets spoke against idolatry but never changed it, we must admit that several godly kings did tear down the strongholds of idolatry. It is not by accident that the book of Revelation declares that Jesus Christ "... has made us kings and priests to His God and Father, to Him be glory and dominion forever and ever. Amen" (Revelation 1:6), and then adds, "[He] ... made us kings and priests to our God; and we shall reign on the earth" (Revelation 5:10). God does not call us to be prophets; He has commissioned us to be kings and has given us authority to reign in life on this earth. The obvious beginning of that reign is in our personal lives. We can take authority in the areas of life He has put into our hands.

Josiah did. After that young king had ascended to the throne of Judah, "when he had broken down the altars and the wooden images, had beaten the carved images into powder, and cut down all the incense altars throughout all the land of Israel, he returned to Jerusalem" (2 Chronicles 34:7). He knew what we must learn. God's Word has the only answer to idols — destroy them! God never instructed His people to bring idols under control. He did not even want the idolaters in Canaan to be made subject to Israel. His universal command was "destroy them." The inhabitants who were spared eventually led Israel into idolatry. King Josiah gave us the only accepted pattern for dealing with idols: tear them down, break them up, burn them and bury the ashes.

God says, "Tear them down."

The first thing Moses did when he saw the golden calf was to tear it down. He pulled it from its pedestal and lowered it from its elevated position. He reduced it to what it was — a lifeless idol. Similarly, the first step God wants us to take with anyone or anything we have allowed to become an idol to us is to take them, or it, off the pedestal. We need to lower these images to our level.

God predicated Gideon's commission to deliver Israel from the Midianites on his obedience to "... tear down the altar of Baal that your father has, and cut down the wooden image that is beside it" (Judges 6:25). There is no indication that Gideon worshiped that idol, but it was part of his heritage — his father had erected it. We need to pull down any idols in our heritage so they can no longer have power over us.

Similarly, Josiah began his reform by breaking down the idols his forefathers had erected. We read: "They broke down the altars of the Baals in his presence, and the incense altars which were above them he cut down ..." (2 Chronicles 34:4) The apostle Paul declared in the New Testament:

For the weapons of our warfare are not carnal but mighty in God for pulling down strongholds, casting down arguments and every high thing that exalts itself against the knowledge of God, bringing every thought into captivity to the obedience of Christ (2 Corinthians 10:4-5).

The weapons God has provided enable us to cast down "every high thing that exalts itself against the knowledge of God."

We must pull down the mental images that books and television programs have created in our minds. It doesn't matter whether our idols are carvings or concepts, they must come down. The Canaanites worshiped pillars and modern Christians worship persons, but God commands us to cast down every form of idolatry. Anything in the holy place of our lives that does not have the life of God in it must go. It is wrong for us to ask God to tear down our idols. The falling down of Dagon is the only biblical example we have of God directly tearing down an idol. God's attitude is, "You built it; you tear it down."

We can remove idolatrous thought patterns from our minds. We can remove persons from their exalted plane whom we have elevated to a godlike position. It won't be easy, because idols can be very resistant to dethroning. They have enjoyed preeminence and have controlled our lives. They may even have become channels for demonic activity within us. Furthermore, others who have joined us in worshiping at our personal altars for sinning will resist our attempts to dismantle them. But those altars must be replaced with the presence of God.

God told Gideon to use a team of oxen to pull down his father's idol. The working ox is also a picture of the Messiah in the Old Testament, as well as one of the four faces of the living creatures. It is also characteristic of the picture of Christ painted by Mark in his gospel. When we initiate action to pull down an idol, Christ Jesus joins that operation. He shares His power and enables us to destroy that idol. Paul said that we have been promised the power of Christ's cross when he wrote:

> *For what the law could not do in that it was weak through the flesh, God did by sending His own Son in the likeness of sinful flesh, on account of sin: He condemned sin in the flesh, that the righteous requirement of the law might be fulfilled in us who do not walk according to the flesh but according to the Spirit* (Romans 8:3-4).

I have known Christians who made such an idol of television that their answer to their idolatry was to sell the television set. I don't condemn them for that. If that is the only way your idol will come down, then do it. Very few of those persons have regretted it; the absence of the television set has forced them to read, to talk to one another, and to play games. Their speech has been cleaned up, and their horizons have been stretched. There are, of course, other ways to handle television. Unplug it or find the "off" switch. No matter how we dethrone it, every idol in our lives *must* be torn down. Merely trying to ignore an idol is only a temporary solution.

God says, "Break them up."

Merely tearing down an idol is insufficient. After Moses tore down the golden calf, he broke it to pieces " ... and ground it to powder" (Exodus 32:20). King Josiah "made dust" (2 Chronicles 34:4) of the carved images, and Gideon broke the Baal idol and the Asterath pillar into pieces. If we leave the idols intact after lowering them from their pedestals, we may not successfully resist the temptation to reinstate them in our lives. We need to grind those idols into powder after we dismantle them so we can be certain there is not even one piece left for a memento. Pulverize those cursed idols.

The psalmist said, "The sacrifices of God are a broken spirit, a broken and a contrite heart — these, O God, You will not despise" (Psalm 51:17). The Hebrew word we translate here as *broken* suggests being crushed, contrited or reduced to powder. The process of making talcum powder beautifully illustrates this concept. Talc stone is broken, ground and pulverized until it will float on water. Thus it is transformed from stone to powder.

Worship requires great inner breaking. It is not that God delights in *our* destruction, but that He wants the idols to which we have given dominion in our lives to be broken until they are useless. Tears in worship may express several things. Sometimes they are but a release of inner frustration. This is valuable and often tranquilizing, but it is not necessarily worship. At other times, tears give evidence of inner sorrow. Perhaps it is the sorrow of being exposed in our idolatry, or maybe it is a longing for the idols we earlier destroyed.

There are times, however, when tears during worship release the pain of the breaking and grinding going on within us. When we see what our idolatry has done to the heart of God, it is almost impossible to maintain a joyful attitude. When the dust of our broken idols gets into our eyes, it may cause them to water uncontrollably. Perhaps we should wear a sign: CAUTION: IDOLS UNDER DESTRUCTION.

Because very few Christians are aware of the inner breaking that is occurring within another, they try to console a crying worshiper. Let them alone. Tears are healing to the soul. I have learned over the years that if I can get a man to cry before God there is a good chance that he can learn to love again. Often what begins as tears of reaction to idol destruction become an expression of deep love for Jesus. God considers weeping before Him so precious that He makes a memorial of our tears. David said of God: "You number my wanderings; put my tears into Your bottle; are they not in Your book?" (Psalm 56:8)

When we determine to break our idols into pieces, our calloused hearts also will break before God. This is a completely positive action. David, who experienced a brokenhearted response to God, said: "The LORD is near to those who have a broken heart, and saves such as have a contrite spirit" (Psalm 34:18). Breakings are redemptive. When we break our idols, God redeems whatever those idols have defiled and devastated.

God says, "Burn them up."

Moses "... took the calf which they had made, burned it in the fire, and ground it to powder ..." (Exodus 32:20) Gideon used the wood of the idol image to build a fire with which to offer a burnt offering to God. Josiah "... brought out the wooden image from the house of the LORD, to the Brook Kidron outside Jerusalem, burned it at the Brook Kidron, and ground it to ashes..." (2 Kings 23:6) These reformers were not content merely to dethrone and destroy an idol. They put the idol's residue into the fire and desired to change its form completely.

John the Baptist said of Jesus: "... He will baptize you with the Holy Spirit and fire" (Matthew 3:11). While these may not be simultaneous actions, they are progressive operations of God's Spirit. Some persons receive the Spirit without the fire action — they need a baptism of love before they can endure God's fire. But the fire will come. Mercifully God's order is first the Spirit's presence, then the Spirit's fire.

When I view the impurity that is evident in the modern Church — the idols that are so obvious — I recognize that many Christians have embraced the love of God and the energy of the Holy Spirit without accepting the fire of God's presence. Whole congregations have come into what they call the "fullness of the Spirit" without experiencing the fullness of the cross of Christ.

Fire speaks of God's nature as surely as love characterizes His being. One definition for Jehovah is "Our God is a consuming fire" (Deuteronomy 4:24; Hebrews 12:29). Ezekiel saw the presence of God as a raging tempest of fire, and God demonstrated His presence at Mt. Sinai with flaming fire. When John, who was banished to the isle of Patmos, saw Christ, he said of Him: "... His eyes [are] like a flame of fire" (Revelation 1:14). From beginning to end, the Bible illustrates a portion of God's nature with the symbol of fire.

The presence of God blesses, but it also burns. Persons often testify that the presence of God produced a burning sensation within them. The fire of God is supernatural, and it will not consume natural material. That is what so amazed Moses at the burning bush. Although the flames ascended through the bush, the bush was never consumed. The fire of God's presence never destroys natural things when it burns. It deals with spiritual substance and is especially destructive to idols.

Fire not only demonstrates an aspect of God's nature, it also speaks of God's purging. Fire was one of God's favorite means of purging sin throughout the Old Testament. The brazen altar, where the priests offered sacrifice for sin, blazed with a flame that God had kindled. After God initiated the fire, He commanded the priests to maintain the flame perpetually. Although the blood of the sacrifice was sprinkled as an atonement for sin, the priests burned the carcass of the holocaust animal for the eradication of sins.

Isaiah experienced an application of this principle when he was caught up into heaven by a vision. When he saw himself before God, who was seated upon His throne, he realized that none of his righteousness came even close to matching the holy nature of Almighty God. He pronounced a woe of judgment declaring himself to be sinful and unholy. God's answer to Isaiah's cry of desperation was to instruct an angel to take a flaming coal from heaven's altar of incense and touch Isaiah's lips. The prophet says: "And he touched my mouth with it, and said: 'Behold, this has touched your lips; your iniquity is taken away, and your sin purged' " (Isaiah 6:7). Fire was, and is, God's agent for purging sin from the lives of believers.

We need not fear the fire action of God's presence, for its purpose is the eradication of the effects of our carnal nature and our past sins. In the Old Testament, defiled instruments could be purged by passing them through fire. In the New Testament economy, the instruments of our whole being can be cleansed and made ceremonially clean by the fire of God's presence.

Fire also speaks of God's judgment. Jesus used the imagery of fire when He spoke of eternal damnation and the final incarceration of satan, his angels and their followers in a "lake of fire" (see Revelation 21:8). Jesus taught that the prince of this world will be judged; He also said that divine judgment begins in the house of God. The most damaging idolatry is practiced in the Church. That is where it needs to be destroyed, not merely dethroned. Our altars to sinning and their idols need to meet the judgment of God's eternal flame until the fire reduces them to harmless ashes.

God says, "Bury the ashes."

Having burned the pieces of the golden calf, Moses scattered the ashes on a pond and caused Israel to drink the water. When Josiah implemented his reforms ...

> *They broke down the altars of the Baals in his presence, and the incense altars which were above them he cut down; and the wooden images, the carved images, and the molded images he broke in pieces, and made dust of them and scattered it on the graves of those who had sacrificed to them* (2 Chronicles 34:4).

Both leaders made it impossible for the people to recover any portion of their idols.

Far too often when we discover that our gold has actually gone into the construction of a golden calf, we try to recover the precious metal. That is not God's way. We cannot reconsecrate anything to Jehovah once we have dedicated it to idols. God wants it to be destroyed. Ashes are worthless for reconstruction. Bury them! Let's treat our idols the way God treats our sins. God forgives our confessed sins, burns them at the brazen altar, and then buries them in the depth of the sea (see Micah 7:19). God will never remember our sins or hold them against us, for He has buried them. They are gone forever.

All altars for sinning separate us from God. The idols we adore at those altars will eventually replace Jehovah as the focus of our devotion, and God will then withdraw His presence from us. We need to take decisive action quickly. We must tear down our idols, break them, burn them and bury the ashes lest our hearts again turn from the true and living God to serve the dead idols we once served.

The few successful reformers in Judah did that. After the idols had been destroyed, the Temple in Jerusalem was repaired and divine worship was reestablished. Although the reformers enforced Jehovah's worship while they lived, after their death the next generation returned to idolatry, rebuilding the idols and the altars to sin.

Since the human heart is the same everywhere, it is likely that after we have done everything we can to destroy our idols and to return to pure worship of God, we will eventually rebuild what we have destroyed unless there is a deep change in our hearts. Some persons seem to spend their entire lives in a cycle of building idols, destroying idols, and rebuilding them again. The outer form changes, but the inner desire remains the same.

We desperately need a work of God's grace to deal with idolatry. While we can deal with the external manifestations, only God can deal with our internal motivations. We can change our deeds, but only God can change our real desires. After we have done everything within our power to rid ourselves of our idols, God's grace does a work in our spirits that purges our consciences to serve a living God. God's grace still enables a person to walk straight in a crooked world.

Little children, keep yourselves from idols. Amen (1 John 5:21).

Chapter 13

The Prevention of Altars for Sinning

It is far more natural to connect idolatry with rebellion than with grace, for the act of idolatry begins with rebellion in the heart. God knows our total inability to forsake idols without the intervention of His grace. That which began as a concept in our minds and progressed to a constraint of our souls soon becomes a compulsion in our spirits.

Behind idols lurk demons intent on receiving our worship and intervening in our affairs. A demonic grip on a person's life can become so strong that no amount of willpower can break it. Idolaters become captives of their idols, and only a stronger power can set that worshiper free. Paul told Titus: "For the grace of God that brings salvation has appeared to all men, teaching us that denying ungodliness and worldly lusts, we should live soberly, righteously, and godly in the present age ..." (Titus 2:11-12) The very power that sets the captive free is **grace**. Without grace there can be neither liberation from the domination of idols nor power to serve God worshipfully.

But grace came! The apostle John heralds this loudly in the prologue to his gospel by saying, "... grace and truth came through Jesus Christ" (John 1:17). When "... the Word became flesh and dwelt among us ... we beheld His glory, the glory as of the only begotten of the Father, full of grace and truth" (John 1:14). Paul testifies that this grace is the active agent in delivering us from the worship of anything short of God. He wrote: "For by grace you have been saved through faith, and that not of yourselves, it is the gift of God" (Ephesians 2:8). He took an even larger step in his letter to the church at Rome when he said, "... where sin abounded, grace abounded much more" (Romans 5:20).

Abounding grace

Abounding grace is God's way of cleansing us from idolatry. What we are unable to do for ourselves, God graciously does for us. God told Judah through Ezekiel: "... I will cleanse you from all your filthiness and from all your idols" (Ezekiel 36:25). God's goal for Judah was not punishment, but purging. He wanted to cleanse His people from the inner compulsion and the outer defilement of idolatry. Only His grace could execute that. When God gave the law to Moses, He promised: "... I will be gracious to whom I will be gracious, and I will have compassion on whom I will have compassion" (Exodus 33:19). God obviously chose to exercise His mercy for His covenant people — and He still does.

All God's dealings with Israel's idolatry were works of grace. His implementation of the Tabernacle worship with its priesthood, sacrifices, rituals and festivals was a gracious provision for the innate cry of the human soul to "worship the LORD in the beauty of holiness" (1 Chronicles 16:29). There was never a genuine need to burn incense to a pagan deity, for the burning of incense before Jehovah was the highest act of worship in the Tabernacle. Idol worship offered nothing of ritual, ceremony or celebration that was lacking in the Tabernacle worship, except sensuality. That worship was divine grace in action. It was God's provision to meet every spiritual drive in the human experience.

When His chosen people sought to satisfy their cravings for worship in idolatrous behavior, God sent the prophets to warn them. He left them neither uninformed nor unchallenged. They did not need to check a history book or even research the law of Moses. God sent His Word to them through His special agents, the prophets. That was abundant grace, for God sent prophet after prophet and confirmed their words with signs. The Hebrews did not reject them as false prophets. They merely considered the message to be unpalatable. In spite of their refusal to heed, God graciously continued to speak to them.

God's grace repeatedly inspired priests to make atonement for the nation. They were often the force behind Judah's revivals, standing as guardians and teachers of the Law. Even when God Himself was not the object of His people's worship, He maintained a relationship of grace with His priests and, through them, with the people.

As we have just seen, God's grace occasionally reached a king who called the people to national repentance and the revitalization of the worship of Jehovah. God's grace was evident in the calling of His people back to Himself through the actions of their kings. When God could no longer reach His people through prophets, priests and kings, He sent them into captivity. Even that was a work of grace. God refused to allow His people to self-destruct. Although the people saw their captivity as *punishment* for their idolatry, God viewed it as a *purging* from their idolatry.

Sometimes when God has been unsuccessful in leading His people out of their sin, He has had to use drastic measures to remove those people from their sinning situations. Such action is not evidence of God's animosity; it is surely a demonstration of His grace. Like a loving parent who forcibly moves a child out of danger after he has refused to respond to instruction, so God demonstrates His lovingkindness to us by bringing us out of our idolatry. Graciously God works from the gentle to the severe. In spite of our failure to respond, God continues to work, because "... He who has begun a good work in [us] will complete it until the day of Jesus Christ" (Philippians 1:6). It is little wonder, then, that the Word declares, "... it is good that the heart be established by grace ..." (Hebrews 13:9)

It is a fallacy to interpret these demonstrations of grace as evidence of our great worth to God. While it is true that we decide the value of an item by the price someone is willing to pay for it, it is equally true that we "... were bought at a price ..." (1 Corinthians 6:20) and "... were not redeemed with corruptible things, like silver or gold ... but with the precious blood of Christ ..." (1 Peter 1:18-19) The price Christ paid to restore us to a worshiping relationship with God does not reflect our worth, either to God or in life. The death of Christ reflects the value God has placed upon His holy name, for every act of grace toward us is for His name's sake. He told Ezekiel: "... I do not do this for your sake, O house of Israel, but for My holy name's sake, which you have profaned among the nations wherever you went" (Ezekiel 36:22). While recounting some of Israel's earlier history, the psalmist said the same thing: "Nevertheless He saved them for His name's sake, that He might make His mighty power known" (Psalm 106:8).

The operation of God's grace in the lives of former idolaters is for His own sake. God did not call Abraham out of idolatry to father the nation of Israel because He recognized great worth in Abraham. God's choice was strictly for His sake. It was for God's purposes. Similarly the progressive work of grace to bring Abraham's progeny out of their self-imposed idolatry was for God's sake. God felt that His reputation was on the line; He refused to let the heathen believe that God was unable to keep the affections of His chosen people.

God's reputation is still on the line. Educators, politicians, scientists and others are looking with disdain at the materialistically oriented Church of today. Since it is obvious to them that we have little respect for Jehovah or His Word, why should they honor and revere the One we have dishonored and against Whom we have rebelled? It would be easy for God to let the Church go her way and begin again with other persons (just as He told Moses He wanted to do after the sin of the golden calf), but God's reputation is at stake.

So God continues to extend grace after grace to His covenant people to bring us out of the world-system into a vital worship relationship with Him. The testimony concerning the early Church said: "... And great grace was upon them all" (Acts 4:33). That active grace kept them from idolatry and allowed God to give them amazing growth and success in a very short time. Since God lives in an eternal now, what He did then, He does yet today. God will yet show this world that He can gather people unto Himself who will obey, serve and lovingly worship Him. For His name's sake, He will bring us out of our idolatry, no matter how painful the workings of His grace may become for us.

Grace in perception

Grace [Greek *charis*] is a small word both in English and in Greek, but its meanings are various. The oldest sense in which ***charis*** is used goes back to Homer who used the word to describe "sweetness" or "attractiveness." From that, it came to mean "favor" and "goodwill." The word was later broadened to mean "lovingkindness," especially when it was shown to an inferior, as by a master to his servant or by a king to his subjects. The New Testament writers adapted the word to express "unearned favor." Paul, however, lifted ***charis*** to new heights and projected it as "God's love in action." He saw grace as a force, power and divine energy given to saints to produce changes in behavior. It was Paul who declared that God has saved us by the action of His grace (see Ephesians 2:8). Paul understood grace to be not only undeserved, but equally unearned and unachievable.

The word ***charis*** occurs about 160 times in the New Testament, where the translators use several English words: favor, thank, pleasure, liberality, benefit, thanks, joy, thankworthy and acceptable. The most common rendering of ***charis*** is **grace**. The New Testament uses the word **grace** in both the objective and the subjective sense. **Objectively** it is what occasions the pleasure, delight or benefit of the recipient. It is the effect of grace or the state of those who have experienced grace. **Subjectively**, grace refers to the friendly disposition from which the kindly acts proceed — or the feeling produced by receiving that grace.

Since New Testament times, we have broadened the word to include: (1) the friendship of God toward men, (2) the gospel generally, especially as opposed to law, (3) certain gifts of God freely bestowed upon His Church, (4) Christian virtues evidenced in personal lives, and (5) the glory yet to be revealed to and in the Church.

Bible readers and students of religious history cannot help being aware that the idea of grace is absolutely foreign to idolatry. While idolaters may desire the favor of their gods, they seldom expect it. They anticipate having to bribe their gods to show them any consideration at all. Although their idols are ever present, there is no perceived closeness between the idolaters and their gods. In the days of Nebuchadnezzar, the king's magicians, astrologers, sorcerers and priests told him, "What the king asks is too difficult. No one can reveal it to the king except the gods, and they do not live among men" (Daniel 2:11, NIV). Because they view their gods as powerful but uncaring, idolaters invest much of their worship energies trying to propitiate the gods. They offer gifts, acts of service, and sacrifices — including human sacrifice — as acts of propitiation. Any idea of propitiation by the god himself is totally foreign to idolaters.

How difficult it must have been for the children of Israel to accept God's provision of a propitiatory (the mercy seat) in the Tabernacle, and to believe that God Himself was making the propitiation for them. Although their four hundred years in Egypt had introduced them to many forms of idolatry, it had never demonstrated grace to them; for disgrace, not grace, is characteristic of idolatry. While grace did not fit the religious scene in which they lived, it did meet the needs of their burdened lives.

Grace in principle

Grace does not originate in the minds of people — it is a revelation from Almighty God. There is nothing in the satanic realm that comes close to matching divine grace, and there is little in the human world that even looks like it. We humans experience compassion for one another, and we can enjoy mutual fondness, but God's grace goes so far beyond anything we possess innately that only spiritual revelation can enable us to grasp it. We do not *perceive* grace through investigation; we *receive* grace because of God's revelation through Jesus Christ.

The apostle Paul was a great exponent of God's grace. He declared that God gave him a dispensation or stewardship of grace (see Ephesians 3:2). He proclaimed grace as a gift of God (see Ephesians 4:7), the basis of our salvation (see Ephesians 2:5,8), a source of spiritual strength for believers (see 2 Timothy 2:1), the very foundation of his being and the reason for his ministry. He wrote:

> For I am the least of the apostles, who am not worthy to be called an apostle, because I persecuted the church of God. But by the grace of God I am what I am, and His grace toward me was not in vain; but I labored more abundantly than they all, yet not I, but the grace of God which was with me (1 Corinthians 15:9-10).

So important had grace become to Paul that he added it to the standard greeting of "peace" in ten of his epistles. "Grace and peace be to you ... " — *charis* and *shalom* — became his salutary opening similar to our "Dear Sir." It is likely that Paul intended it as a benediction or an impartation, for nothing he could write would be more valuable than a touch of God's great grace.

I know of no published works on idolatry that offer this impartation to the worshipers. Where is the loving benediction of their gods? The scriptures never mentioned it. Grace is an area where God, through Christ Jesus, holds a complete monopoly. That is why grace must be received by faith, for it is foreign to our innate natures.

Grace is integrally wrapped up in the very nature of God. The New Testament uses the expression "grace of God," or "grace of our Lord Jesus" nearly 40 times. The Old Testament calls Jehovah a "gracious" God nearly 25 times. When Jonah purchased a one-way ticket to

Tarshish instead of going to Nineveh as directed, he explained his action by saying to God, "... for I know that You are a gracious and merciful God, slow to anger and abundant in lovingkindness, One who relents from doing harm" (Jonah 4:2). Jonah knew that God's nature of grace would override His threat of punishment.

After one of Israel's severe rebellions in which the people threatened to stone Moses to death, God appeared in the cloud of glory and told Moses to step aside and let Him slay the congregation. God said that He would gladly start all over with the sons of Moses. While interceding with God, Moses quoted the description that God had given of Himself to Moses on Mt. Sinai. Moses prayed, "... let the power of my Lord be great, just as You have spoken, saying, 'The LORD is longsuffering and abundant in mercy, forgiving iniquity and transgression ...'" (Numbers 14:17-18) Moses pleaded the gracious nature of God and overrode the threatenings of an angry God.

The concept of grace is completely inseparable from the nature of God Himself. **Grace** is what God is, not merely something He exercises. The psalmists frequently wrote: "The Lord is gracious and full of compassion" (Psalm 111:4; 86:15; 112:4). Peter, who experienced great grace after the resurrection of Jesus, viewed all grace as originating in God. He wrote: "The God of all grace, Who called us to His eternal glory by Christ Jesus ... " He sensed that God's grace formed part of His divine image.

In the New Testament, we have four definitions of the nature of God: (1) "God is light" (1 John 1:5), (2) "God is love" (1 John 4:8), (3) God is holy (1 Peter 1:16), and (4) "God is a consuming fire" (Hebrews 12:28). These definitions of God describe energy. *Light* is the source of all natural energy used in our world, *love* is the emotional energy that gives meaning to this life, *holiness* is spiritual energy that gives direction to life, and *fire* transforms energy from one form to another — from a solid substance to heat and light. Since these fundamental definitions of God all speak of energy sources, would not the grace of God also speak of energy? God's grace is a force, a power, an energy that transforms the human life and brings persons back into a proper relationship with God. Little wonder, then, that when Paul was in the midst of much persecution and the buffeting of a messenger of satan, the Lord said to him, "... My grace is sufficient for you, for My strength is made perfect in weakness" (2 Corinthians 12:9). Those who have received divine grace have received sufficient life and energy to face anything the world, the flesh or the devil can bring against them.

Grace in practice

The destruction of Jerusalem with its Temple and the enslavement of Judah into Babylonian captivity was a terrible price to pay for idolatry. But it was more a work of God's grace than a sentence of judgment. In the midst of their captivity, God spoke to His people through His prophet and said:

> *For I will take you from among the nations, gather you out of all countries, and bring you into your own land. Then I will sprinkle clean water on you, and you shall be clean; I will cleanse you from all your filthiness and from all your idols. I will give you a new heart and put a new spirit within you; I will take the heart of stone out of your flesh and give you a heart of flesh. I will put My Spirit within you and cause you to walk in My statutes, and you will keep My judgments and do them. Then ... you shall be My people, and I will be your God. I will deliver you from all your uncleannesses* (Ezekiel 36:24-29).

What a demonstration of abounding grace! God offered **repossession:** "I will ... bring you into your own land"; **remission:** "I will cleanse you from all your filthiness"; **removal:** "I will cleanse you ... from all your idols"; **regeneration:** "I will give you a new heart"; **revelation:** "I will put My Spirit within you"; **reformation:** "I will ... cause you to walk in My statutes"; and **restoration:** "You shall be My people, and I will be your God." That is far more than a kindly feeling on God's part or an undeserved favor toward His people. That was love in action — the energy of grace transforming lives. That is grace at work!

Neither God nor His grace has changed since He spoke that prophecy to Judah. God's grace is still an active force in the lives of believers. In actual Christian behavior, God's grace works on three levels. There is grace to **know**, grace to **will**, and grace to **do** the will of God.

It is only through revelation that we can know the sin of idolatry. Because idolatry is an act of worship, it masquerades as a righteous, holy action. It is religious, it is emotional, and it involves a release of devotion. How could we see this as sin? It is not until the Holy Spirit reveals to us the **object** of our worship that we can begin to see that everything we did, no matter how devoted or sincere we may have been, was sin because the receiver of our adoration was not Jehovah God.

We dare not trust our feelings or even our mental censorship. We need the discerning work of the indwelling Holy Spirit. He will be quick to tell us that our giving is not going to God, or that we have turned our adoration upon ourselves. The Spirit is both willing and able to reveal to us whatever adjustment we need to make until our worship is acceptable to God and beneficial to us. Paul reminds us:

For those who live according to the flesh set their minds on the things of the flesh, but those who live according to the Spirit, the things of the Spirit. For to be carnally minded is death, but to be spiritually minded is life and peace. Because the carnal mind is enmity against God; for it is not subject to the law of God, nor indeed can be. So then, those who are in the flesh cannot please God (Romans 8:5-8).

Although we know neither the secret thoughts of our hearts nor the mind of God, the indwelling Spirit knows them perfectly. Fortunately, He delights in sharing that knowledge with us. What an abundant resource is ours through the Holy Spirit.

Such knowledge is the work of God's grace. God does not intend for us to learn to worship by trial and error. He has imparted His Spirit to teach us what is right and what is wrong in our worship. Just as He told Judah, "... the nations shall know that I am the LORD ... when I am hallowed in you before their eyes" (Ezekiel 36:23), so God extends His great grace to keep Himself before our eyes and to show His presence to others who look at us.

If God merely extended grace to know, we would be blessed; but He has also pledged Himself to send us the grace to **will**. The New Testament places far more emphasis on our desires than on our deeds. As long as we continue to seek satisfaction for the cry of our spirit in something short of God, we will change only the **object** of our worship, not the **obsession** to worship it. While this fixation can be redirected, it is very difficult to restrict it completely.

The attitude of the people left in Judah after its capture by Nebuchadnezzar illustrates the strength of that inner craving after idols. Those people had seen the extreme judgments of God upon Israel and Judah. They had watched as the armies destroyed their idols, cut down their high places, and even burned the Temple. If anyone could have understood the fallacy of idolatry, it should have been them. But in spite of what they had seen, they still approached Jeremiah with the announcement that they were returning to the worship of the goddess of heaven. They irrationally attributed the calamities they had experienced to the abandonment of that worship and reasoned that returning to idol worship would bring them back to prosperity and peace. They knew what was right, but the desires of their hearts overruled the logic of their minds. They reacted to their feelings instead of their faith.

The New Testament says: "... for it is God who works in you both to will and to do for His good pleasure" (Philippians 2:13). By the operation of His great grace, God first changes our will, which, in turn, redirects our wants. When we allow God to adjust our will, He controls our behavior without violating our free moral agency.

That is our only hope of completely abandoning idolatry. A complete change of attitude and desire by sheer willpower is difficult. Few persons in our generation have developed the discipline to consistently refuse to return to their idols, no matter how meaningless they may have proved to be. Paul was well aware of the conflict between knowing right and doing it. He wrote:

> ... For what I will to do, that I do not practice; but what I hate, that I do. ... For the good that I will to do, I do not do; but the evil I will not to do, that I practice. Now if I do what I will not to do, it is no longer I who do it, but sin that dwells in me. ... For I delight in the law of God according to the inward man. But I see another law in my members, warring against the law of my mind, and bringing

me into captivity to the law of sin which is in my members (Romans 7:15,19-20,22-23).

While this is difficult to read, it is very easy to relate to. All have faced this problem. Like Paul, we cry out, "O wretched man that I am! Who will deliver me from this body of death? I thank God — through Jesus Christ our Lord!" (Romans 7:24-25) Our only deliverance is through the grace of God that came in Jesus Christ.

When we allow God's grace to change our hearts and write divine principles upon our inner persons, then we can abandon our idols, forsake our sin, and return to the pure worship of the Lord Jesus Christ. To have a revelation of our idolatry is one thing, but to have a release from its power is still another. God has authorized His grace to do both of these for and in us. His grace enables us to know, and that same grace causes us to will, what is right in the light of that knowledge.

God's grace has not come to replace us. There is always human participation in divine stimulation. God's grace works in us to will us to do God's good pleasure, but the activation of that will is still up to us. God does not treat us like preprogrammed robots. He deals with us as sons and daughters. His grace reveals what is right, motivates us to move into what is right, and then offers us His assistance to do what is right. But He will not compel us, nor will He completely do it for us.

God told Judah,

I will put My Spirit within you and cause you to walk in My statutes, and you will keep My judgments and do them. Then you shall dwell in the land that I gave to your fathers; you shall be My people, and I will be your God (Ezekiel 36:27-28).

When looking at a future restoration, the visionary prophet Zechariah wrote, "I will pour on the house of

David and on the inhabitants of Jerusalem the **Spirit of grace** and supplication; ... in that day there shall be a great mourning in Jerusalem ..." (Zechariah 12:10-11) He who was previously called "My Spirit" is now called "Spirit of grace," and when He is poured out, we mourn over our sin. The context reveals how personal that mourning becomes. It is difficult for any of us to have a sufficient understanding of sin to grieve over it until the Spirit of grace comes to us. He not only reveals sin in its hideousness, but He also causes us to want freedom from it. Thus He motivates us to repent and forsake it.

It is this action of the Spirit that prepares us for the higher work God desires to do. Zechariah continues the account:

> *In that day a fountain shall be opened for the house of David and for the inhabitants of Jerusalem, for sin and for uncleanness. "It shall be in that day" says the LORD of hosts, "that I will cut off the names of the idols from the land, and they shall no longer be remembered. I will also cause the prophets and the unclean spirit to depart from the land"* (Zechariah 13:1-2).

True repentance begins as a work of the Spirit of grace, but it must be released in complete honesty before the throne of God. When we do this, God cuts off the very names of the idols we worshiped and causes the unclean spirits that had enticed us into idolatry to flee from our lives and homes.

While it is obvious that we want to serve God, and equally apparent that we have difficulty remaining pure in our service, God has made grace available to us. His grace will enable us to know, to will and to do for His good pleasure. Perhaps, then, the first step in the abandoning of idolatry is to "... let us have grace by which we may serve God ..." (Hebrews 12:28)

Little children, keep yourselves from idols. Amen
(1 John 5:21).

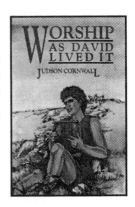

SECRETS OF THE MOST HOLY PLACE

by Don Nori.

Here is a prophetic parable you will read again and again. The winds of God are blowing, drawing you to His Life within the Veil of the Most Holy Place. There you begin to see as you experience a depth of relationship your heart has yearned for. This book is a living, dynamic experience with God!

TPB-182p. ISBN 1-56043-076-1
Retail $8.99

**A TIME TO DANCE:
AN INVITATION**
by Barbara Knoll.
The biblical dance is a lifestyle
not limited to movement with
music, yet such movement is
an exciting expression of our
worship to the Lord. This is a
passionate call for a heart that
dances before the Lord, both in
movement and in relationship
to Him.
TPB-112p. ISBN 1-56043-703-0
Retail $7.99

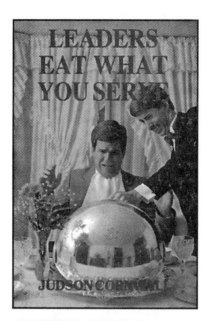

LEADERS: EAT WHAT YOU SERVE

by Judson Cornwall.

This book is written with scholarship, compassion, and truth. Despite the pressures and demands of ministry, leaders must apply to themselves what they share with others to find the strength, direction, and grace to fulfill the work of the ministry. TPB-238p. ISBN 0-914903-59-4 Retail $7.99